Issues in Education

GENERAL EDITOR: PHILIP HILLS

Education and the Teacher Unions

Other Books in This Series

Michael Barber

Education and the
Teacher Unions

NOT power over curriculum
during the '70's (p 43)

CASSELL

Cassell
Villiers House
41/47 Strand
London WC2N 5JE

First published 1992

British Library Cataloguing in Publication Data
Barber, Michael
    Education and the teacher unions. – (Issues
in education)
    I. Title   II. Series
    331.88113711

ISBN 0–304–32359–4 (hardback)
    0–304–32364–0 (paperback)

Library of Congress Cataloging-in-Publication Data
Barber, Michael, 1955–
    Education and the teacher unions / Michael Barber.
       p.   cm. – (Issues in education)
    Includes bibliographical references and index.
    ISBN 0–304–32359–4 – ISBN 0–304–32364–0 (pbk.)
    1. National Union of Teachers – History.   2. Teachers' unions –
England – History.   3. Teachers' unions – Wales – History.   I. Title.
II. Series: Issues in education (London, Eng.)
    LB2844.53.G7B37   1992
    331.88'113711'00942 – dc20   91–3241
                                                                    CIP

Typeset by Fakenham Photosetting Limited, Fakenham, Norfolk
Printed and bound in Great Britain by Biddles Ltd, Guildford and King's
Lynn

Contents

Foreword: The purpose of this series

The educational scene is changing rapidly. This change is being caused by a complexity of factors which includes a re-examination of present educational provision against a background of changing social and economic policies, the 1988 Education Reform Act, new forms of testing and assessment, a National Curriculum, and local management of schools with more participation by parents.

As the educational process is concerned with every aspect of our lives and our society both now and for the future, it is of vital importance that all teachers, teachers in training, administrators and educational policy-makers should be aware and informed on current issues in education.

This series of books is thus designed to inform on current issues, to look at emerging ones, and to give an authoritative overview which will be of immense help to all those involved in the education process.

Philip Hills
Cambridge

Preface

A few words of explanation are necessary about what this book is and what it is not. It provides an interpretation of the history of the National Union of Teachers (NUT), the largest British teacher union. It also offers an analysis of the way in which a teacher union such as the NUT attempts to influence policy on behalf of its members. It examines the current academic debate about the future development of teacher unionism. Finally, relating the analysis closely to the post-Education Reform Act conditions in England and Wales, it makes tentative suggestions about the direction teacher unionism in this country might take in the 1990s.

It is not a detailed history of the NUT in the way that Asher Tropp's book was in the last generation (Tropp, 1957). In particular, I have tried to select the underlying themes of the Union's history, though in a largely narrative framework, rather than providing a blow-by-blow account. One consequence of this is that many outstanding individuals who made major contributions to the Union's development do not appear in the history. I hope they will forgive me.

The book is focused solely on England and Wales, and largely on the NUT. In the historical chapters, the other teacher organizations are only mentioned when they are essential to the story of the NUT. This is not intended to imply that some or all of them have not made important contributions to the development of teaching and education. It is partly to keep the book within manageable limits and partly because, as an employee of the NUT, I felt it would be invidious for me to make judgements, where they could be avoided, on rival teacher organizations. Much of the analysis, however, may be relevant to them as well: whether it is or not is for them and their members to decide.

It must be said that the book is not in any sense an official NUT publication. The selections, the interpretations and the analysis are solely mine. However, given my long association with the Union, both as a member or as an employee, it would surprise me if – hard though I have tried – there were no bias. I state that now so that readers can judge for themselves. One bias I am completely conscious of – and admit to at the outset – is that I do believe that teacher organizations have made, and will continue to make, an important and largely positive contribution to the development of publicly provided education in the UK.

A book of this sort naturally draws on information and ideas not only from the written sources which can be acknowledged, but also from conversations with a wide range of people. I wish to acknowledge specifically a number of individuals and groups. D.A. Howell and Pam Young at the Institute of Education, London, were unfailingly helpful. I benefited greatly from discussing aspects of the work with Martin Lawn and Chapter 5 with Duncan MacFarlane. Tanya Kreisky, who word-processed the text and sorted out the references, also provided a number of highly perceptive comments and criticisms on the overall style and content. Janet Friedlander assisted with sources and the index. Inspiration came from the many Union people – Executive members, Division and Association officers, members in general – I meet in my work, from fellow students on my part-time MA course, from colleagues at NUT headquarters and, above all, from staff past and present in the Education and Equal Opportunities Department, where it is my pleasure to work. I am grateful to, and full of admiration for, all of these people. However, responsibility for the views expressed and for any faults in the book rests with me alone.

Introduction

[Teachers have] too exalted a notion of their own position and of what they have to do. *(Sir Frederick Temple to the Newcastle Commission, 1863)*

When Sir Frederick Temple argued in 1863 that teachers had 'too exalted a notion' of their role, he was expressing a view which was widely shared among the Victorian ruling class; it is a view which has never entirely been eradicated. Teachers have therefore found a need, since the mid-Victorian era, for organizations which represent their views collectively and which advocate not only worthwhile salaries and decent conditions, but also a view of teaching as a profession of importance, status and value to society; furthermore, they have found that these two central aims are not contradictory or alternative, but inextricably related. The more effectively they can convince government and the public that teaching is of value, the more likely they are to see investment in education and hence in their salaries and conditions of service; and vice versa. In short, if teacher unions are to serve their members – which is after all the reason for their existence – they must counter the Frederick Temples of this world and promote the view that teaching is indeed a role of which it is right to have an exalted notion.

After a decade in which trade unions in general, and teacher unions in particular, have been under attack from the government, it may seem either provocative or perhaps merely foolhardy to speak of 'an exalted notion'. The 1980s, after all, saw a steady diminution of teacher union involvement in national policy-making. The Schools' Council, on which they had been the dominant influence, was abolished in 1983; the Advisory Committee on the Supply and Education of Teachers was 'stood down' in 1985; and the Burnham Committee, which had negotiated teachers' salaries for over sixty years, was legislated out of existence in 1987.

Furthermore, the decade also saw perhaps the bitterest dispute over teachers' pay in history, a dispute which left all of the teacher organizations facing a series of profound questions about both their purposes and the methods by which they might achieve them. The similarity of the problems they faced, however, did little to bring them together and disunity remained at the end of the decade, as it had been at the beginning, a bugbear to many in the profession.

Above all, as the education sector moved into the 1990s, it was in the process of being transformed by a series of reforms which virtually all the teacher organizations had fiercely contested and bitterly opposed. Teacher 'ownership' of change was part of the professional jargon, but it did not apply to the reality. In place of the partnership between organized teachers, local authorities and central government which had underpinned the post-war settlement, the government imposed a structure which was governed on the one hand by a centralization of power, and on the other by giving free rein to market forces. The government would control the framework and the curriculum; within this framework schools would compete, one with another, for resources and 'achievement'.

Part of the rationale for this upheaval was precisely to reduce the influence of teacher unions, which were characterized along with local education authorities and teacher educators as part of a cosy educational establishment dedicated to pursuing its self-interest at the expense of children's achievement. The success of the government in bludgeoning the 1988 Education Reform Act on to the statute book, in spite of the almost united opposition of this establishment, could be seen – perhaps the government saw it so – as the death knell for the idea of the teacher unions as 'the mightiest lever of educational reform', as Sir George Kekewich, the senior civil servant at the Board of Education, had described the NUT in the 1890s (Tropp, 1957, p. 270).

Ironically, however, once the government started to

implement its reforms, it began to discover the importance of winning the support of teachers. Indeed, by 1991, the perception that without such support the reforms would fail had led government ministers to make a series of concessions – on the prescriptiveness of the National Curriculum and on the nature of assessment, for example – which had never been envisaged by the framers of the Act. This acknowledgement of the importance of teachers, if sustained, would give leverage to their unions and demonstrate their continuing influence.

A variety of social and economic forces, some of which are beyond the control of national government, are likely to augment that leverage in the decade ahead. The severe shortage of teachers, which is partly a consequence of government education policy, results also from the growing demand for graduates in the industrial and commercial sector and a rapid increase in salary levels for them. Unless the government chooses to reduce substantially the quality of entrants to the profession, which it is clearly considering, it will have to meet long-standing union objectives both on salaries and on equal opportunities for women teachers.

Similarly, the shift in management styles across the progressive elements of industry and commerce towards flatter, more collaborative approaches will undoubtedly eventually affect government education policy; indeed, the School Management Task Force Report (1989) already bears the marks of such influence. Such development could again enable unions to achieve their objective of giving every teacher a voice in school-level decision-making.

More powerful than all of these, however, is the growing evidence that the UK's economic future depends on the development of an education service which ensures achievement for everyone. The pace of change on the brink of the new millennium is such that it is essential to ensure that, as young people become adults, they have the confidence and the desire to continue to learn and re-learn throughout life. It has been argued in a McKinsey survey that, by the year 2000, 70 per cent of jobs in Europe will require cerebral, as opposed to manual, skills (Handy, 1989). An education system designed to provide for an elite cannot meet that challenge. This, again, could make it possible for teacher unions to achieve long-cherished aims, not least the recognition by government that substantial investment in education is not a drain on the economy but, on the contrary, a prerequisite of its success.

For all these reasons, therefore, I believe it can be argued that the influence of teacher unions, far from being in decline, could increase substantially during the 1990s. Such an increase is, however, by no means inevitable. It depends on decisions teacher unions make on their objectives, and on how they seek to achieve them. In highly democratic organizations, like the NUT, such decisions will be the subject of widespread debate.

This book sets out to inform that debate by:

(i) examining the influence of a teacher union on the policy-making process;

(ii) exploring how the nature of that influence, and the means by which it is achieved, has changed over time; and

(iii) examining the current academic debate on the subject and, by drawing some conclusions from that, exploring some possible future options for a teacher union such as the NUT.

The content of the book is based almost entirely on secondary sources. The debt, throughout its historical analysis, to Asher Tropp, Martin Lawn, R.D. Coates and, to a lesser extent, Walter Roy and Peter Gosden should be acknowledged. However, a number of original government and NUT sources have been consulted, normally in the course of confirming generalizations or assertions made by one of the secondary sources. In the sections on the 1980s and 1990–1 there is information based on publicly available NUT papers. These are not acknowledged individually, but have normally been a helpful source of examples to support argumentation. NUT publications on which the argument depends, such as *A Strategy for the Curriculum* (NUT, 1990a) are acknowledged in the same way as other sources.

While, therefore, the book contains little original research, it does attempt to develop an original approach to teacher unions in England and Wales by drawing on the research of others, and by examining in depth the emerging and important debate about whether there is a 'new teacher unionism'.

The first five chapters of the book provide a sweeping narrative history of the NUT. Analysis is woven into the text, and plays an increasingly important part in the final historical chapter, which brings the story through to the present. Because of its importance to the current climate of education and teacher unionism, the history of the pay dispute of the mid-1980s is examined in more depth than other aspects of recent teacher union history.

Chapter 6 explores the means which teacher unions, and the NUT in particular, use in their attempts to exercise influence. This is examined within a framework provided at the start of the chapter by an analysis of the concept of power.

Chapter 7 deals with the debate so far about a new teacher unionism. It looks at a number of established studies of the teacher union influence in this country. It also examines the international debate on the future of teacher unions, and explores in particular the extremely important work of Charles Kerchner and Douglas Mitchell, *The Changing Idea of a Teachers' Union* (1988). This debate is, in my view, only just beginning, at any rate in the United Kingdom. The chapter therefore concludes with an examination of how a teacher union in the UK might approach the conditions it is likely to face in the 1990s. As I have suggested above, this is intended not only to provoke a new phase of academic debate about teacher unionism, but also, and more importantly, to give members of teacher unions around the country access to that debate. Ultimately, after all, it is teachers as union members who will decide the future of their organizations and the extent to which they can justify an exalted notion of their role.

For Karen

1 The origins of the NUT, 1870–1910

The preconditions

By the end of the 1860s the need for an organization which could defend and promote the interests of teachers was palpable. That decade had been dominated, as far as teachers were concerned, by the implementation of the detested and bitterly opposed Revised Code. The Code brought an end to any direct payments from the state to teachers or pupil teachers, removed any rights they had to a pension and abolished a range of grants that had been available to schools. Instead, it provided for grants to be made to school managers, the level of which depended on the attendance of pupils and their success in examinations – carried out by external inspectors – in each of the 'three Rs'. How this grant was spent was a matter for the manager, often the local vicar, to determine. Hence, a teacher's salary, tenure and conditions were at the mercy of the school manager, while the curriculum that a teacher taught was prescribed nationally in the Code. (The reader in the 1990s could hardly fail to notice the striking similarity between this and some of the thinking behind the 1988 Education Reform Act.) It was difficult to see how the teaching profession could have been ground any further down.

Two great pillars of Victorian ideology made possible the implementation of the Revised Code. On the one hand was the view that the state should spend, and regulate affairs, as little as possible, while as much as possible should be left to the operation of the laws of supply and demand. Hence the decision to cut direct payments to teachers. On the other hand was the view that the children of the working classes – the vast majority –

should be prevented from becoming 'overeducated'. It was economically beneficial for them to acquire basic numeracy and literacy; it was socially valuable for them to receive a dose of paternalistic religious education; more than that was dangerous. Among some of the middle class the two arguments ran neatly together: 'surely it is unjust to force the middle classes to pay for educating the children of the masses more than they can afford to educate their own,' complained J.C. Wigram in 1849 (Tropp, 1957, p. 59).

The success of the Revised Code's proponents taught many teachers an important lesson, echoes of which are almost as loud now as the original lesson was then; the divisions among them played into the hands of those who not only feared the overeducation of pupils but also believed that teachers themselves were overeducated and beginning to get ideas above their station. Leaving aside the teachers in the public schools and the schools of the middle class, who in any case wished to keep their distance from elementary teachers well into this century, the chief divisions among teachers were on religious grounds.

During the debates around the 1870 Education Act, teachers were able to recognize that the growing importance of secular education ought to make it possible for them to minimize their differences. They accepted that the lessons of the Bible could be taught in a non-denominational way, and that a conscience clause could allow children whose parents desired it to opt out of lessons for religious instruction.

These compromises made possible the creation of a union for all elementary teachers regardless of religion, and in June 1870 the National Union of Elementary Teachers was founded.

The development of the NUT, 1870–1910

It is worth noting that at the outset the NUT, known as the NUET until 1889, was a national union (though its local associations had, and still have, extensive autonomy), founded in response to decisions taken at national level, such as the introduction of the Revised Code. This is in stark contrast to most of the industrial and craft unions which developed in the second half of the nineteenth century, which generally emerged as amalgamations or federations of local or company-focused unions. As a consequence the NUT has, both tactically and strategically, placed great weight on its dealings with national government throughout its history, and has never suffered to the same extent from the geographical divisions which have plagued unions such as the mineworkers'.

The fact that the NUT was founded in the same year as the Foster Education Act was passed is no coincidence. In classic Victorian style the Act established a national system of elementary education 'at least cost with least loss of voluntary help and greatest possible aid from parents' (Batho, 1989, p. 7). It did so by establishing school boards to provide elementary education on the rates where voluntary societies were unable or unwilling to do so. From the beginning, therefore, the NUT had to deal on two levels: with the Board of Education at national level on education and employment policy; and at school-board or voluntary-school level, where the employer was located. Ever since, the NUT has had both to deal effectively at these two levels and to make policy decisions about which powers it wants located at which level. Throughout its history runs a deep mistrust of overcentralized state power in education policy, a mistrust which manifests itself today in conflict over, for example, the history curriculum. On the other hand, without intervention by the state the dangers of uneven investment and shoddy policy implementation are ever present. Hence the current opposition to local pay bargaining and the constant struggles in the late nineteenth century with school boards whose only ambition was to keep the rates down.

The arguments on which the early NUT based its case remain for the most part the arguments today. Then as now the force of the Union's case was that what is good for teachers is good for children, or, as the NUT's first president J.J. Graves put it, 'by the elevation of the teacher, we elevate the value of education, and accelerate the progress of civilisation' (Tropp, 1957, p. 108).

Much of the early work of the Union was on the basic themes of all trade unions; tenure, salaries, conditions of service, superannuation and control of entry to the profession. These are both straightforward trade union aims and professional aims. In the late nineteenth century no contradiction between the two was perceived. When teachers argued at that time for registration of certified teachers and for teacher control over entry to the profession they were well aware of the success of doctors and lawyers in this respect half a century earlier. They were also clearly pursuing their own self-interest, since they rightly took the view that levels of salary would ultimately be determined by the supply of, and demand for, teachers, and as long as the government determined supply and demand, it would also control salaries. The idea that 'a profession' involves putting the interests of the client before those of the professional overlooks an important fact: that in the established professions it is because the interests of the professional are so well taken care of that the client can be put first. Those who, throughout history, have accused teachers of putting self-interest first would do well to remember how precarious teachers' salaries and conditions have been at times.

The early NUT had a varying success rate with these employment issues. Repeated deputations to the Board of Education failed to achieve security of tenure. Since teachers, particularly in rural areas, were employed at the pleasure of the employer, often the vicar, security of tenure was a major concern. On appointment, a new vicar would often want to replace the incumbent teacher and could do so. The strength of the Union with its legal department was an asset to teachers in such situations and, while it failed to change national policy, the Union had increasing success at local level. The Union also fought for a right of appeal to the Board in cases where the inspector, under the 'payment by results' system, put the teacher in jeopardy. Certificated teachers could lose their certificate or be blacklisted by the Department of Education in such cases. Only in the 1890s, when George Kekewich became the Permanent Secretary at the Board and struck up a close relationship with the Union's General Secretary, James Yoxall, was a right of appeal granted in cases of withdrawal of the certificate.

Whereas industrial unions, such as the dockers', had increasing success in the late nineteenth century in their direct pursuit of increased wages, the NUT set out to raise salaries indirectly by controlling supply. They had little success before 1910, partly because the Department was ever willing to flood the system with untrained, uncertificated teachers, who were cheaper and until 1919 not organized by the NUT; and partly because it became increasingly obvious that many of the employers, particularly the voluntary schools in rural areas, could only afford to pay meagre salaries. The rural school boards – often dominated by farmers who, in any case, saw children as cheap labour and school therefore as a distraction – exacerbated the difficulty by setting out only to keep the rates down. Hence by the start of the twentieth century the Union's salary ambitions were promoted by demands both for a Teachers' Registration Council, which would control supply, and for a new Education Act, which would provide greater state aid to voluntary schools and rural areas.

With regard to teachers' conditions, the Union's main campaign was against 'extraneous duties'. Class sizes of sixty or so, it seems, were of less concern than teachers being required to play the organ in church on Sunday. An NUT survey in 1891 found that 400 teachers, out of 1200 questioned, depended for their employment on extraneous duties such as running Sunday school or training the church choir. Attempts to persuade the Department that this represented not only an imposition on teachers, but also in effect a squandering of public money on purposes for which it was never intended, foundered on the age-old plea of the Department that if it acted on this matter, it would represent a dangerous extension of central interference. Nevertheless, the creation of local education authorities (LEAs) and the increased formalization of the education service after 1902 resulted eventually in such practices withering away.

On superannuation, the Union eventually had greater success. As early as 1846, teachers had been granted a pension entitlement, but increasing concern at the cost to the state led this to be whittled away during the 1850s and scrapped altogether by the Revised Code. Consistent pressure by the Union from its earliest days was rewarded in the 1898 Superannuation Act, which restored a pension entitlement for teachers.

The Union's fundamental strategic aim, 'the establishment of a teaching profession on a par with doctors', was not achieved. T.E. Heller, the Union's second General Secretary, explained both the problem and the Union's proposed solution in a speech in 1878. Teachers were burdened with 'the responsibilities and trammels of state service ... while all the advantages of such service have been denied or withdrawn' (Tropp, 1957, p. 115). To rectify this he proposed that 'the power of controlling entrance into the profession must be placed in the hands of an independent representative body under the control of Parliament, and the teacher's diploma must be placed beyond the caprice or the necessities of a government department' (*ibid.*). Concern today about licensed teachers could not have been more crisply put.

When a Teachers' Registration Council was finally established by Act of Parliament in 1907, its powers were limited, and it was scuppered by resistance from the Board of Education and its imperious Permanent Secretary Robert Morant. He was able throughout to manipulate the divisions between the different teacher associations – particularly the gulf between the elementary and the grammar-school teachers – which had undermined the hierarchical 1899 register that separated elementary teachers from others. As a result, the Teachers' Registration Council was never more than an irrelevance.

Nevertheless, in spite of this failure, the early NUT campaigned with some success on wider 'professional' and educational issues. It pursued vigorously, for example, one element of becoming an established profession – the control of its own inspection. Under the Revised Code, inspection was imposed from outside, since its framers believed that elementary teachers were in need not only of inspection but also of control, so that the 'overeducation' of the working class could be prevented. Hence inspectors, with all their draconian power under the Code, were often 'young men ... fresh from the university, who [had] never seen the inside of a public elementary school' (quoted in Tropp, 1957, p. 119).

The Union pressed for the recruitment of inspectors from among elementary teachers, both because it believed this would improve the quality of inspection, and also as an opportunity for career advancement for its members. It met, however, with little success. Sixty 'inspector's assistants' were appointed, but they had little power. In 1882 a sub-inspectorate was established and between 1894 and 1902 six ex-elementary teachers were promoted, via this route, to the full inspectorate; but even this modest rate of success was brought to a halt in 1901 by the creation of 'junior inspectors', all recruited from Oxford and Cambridge, to replace the sub-inspectorate.

By contrast, on the central educational issue of the late nineteenth century, payment by results, the NUT met with complete success. No other organization maintained such implacable opposition to it. Since the Code was revised annually, the Union was presented with regular opportunities to intervene. Each year it would promote certain modifications to the Code, though it never relaxed its opposition to the system as a whole. The campaign against it reached its peak in the 1880s with teachers, led by the Union, arguing that the system was damaging education by 'stringing up' demands on teachers and causing 'overpressure'. The 1880 Code brought in by Mundella required a 100 per cent pass rate if schools were to receive their full grant. Concessions to the teachers made by Mundella in 1882 and 1883 were withdrawn in 1884/5, Mundella having resigned when the 'over-pressure' controversy was at its peak.

Then, as later, such campaigns provided dilemmas for the

7

Union. Its case was that 'over-pressure' reduced the quality of education, but its campaign also provided sustenance to those who believed that publicly provided education for working-class children was over-rated in any case. Hence the Conservatives in the 1880s turned the 'over-pressure' controversy into an attack on 'overeducation' in general.

In fact the Union's line in the controversy appears in the long run to have been successful. Two years after his resignation, Mundella condemned the system of payment by results. The Cross Commission split on the issue. Finally, the appointment of George Kekewich to head the Board led to the system's abolition. By 1895 the dreaded annual exam was only administered in cases where a school was already perceived to be falling below acceptable standards.

The Union had other notable successes. Elementary education was made compulsory in 1880 and fees in provided (as opposed to voluntary) schools were abolished in 1881. Campaigns on behalf of the 'half-timer' and those who, through ill health or poor nutrition, were unable to take advantage of education also bore fruit in the early twentieth century. Perhaps most important of all is the evidence that, throughout the time of the Revised Code, many teachers continued to provide their pupils with an education broader than that which the Code required. Most elementary teachers of the time had their roots firmly in the working class and saw the importance of education to their pupils exactly as their opponents who fought against 'overeducation' did, though they drew opposite conclusions.

The NUT's view of the need for a coherent education system, with 'an educational ladder' to secondary and technical education, clear links between elementary, secondary and university education, and teacher training firmly embedded in the system, can also be seen to have influenced the 1902 Education Act. Its more ambitious goals had to await 1944. The 1902 Act swept away the old school boards, many of which had been tiny, and gave responsibility for educational provision to the county and county borough councils. Hence local education authorities became part of local authorities with a multiplicity of other functions. They were given the power to provide not only elementary education, but also secondary, technical and teacher education. Furthermore, as the Union had proposed, teachers' salaries – even in voluntary schools – were now to become the responsibility of the LEAs, as was the power of dismissal. As a result the vagaries of the local vicar, the rural voluntary school and the small school board passed into history.

While many of the LEAs remained keen to keep the rates down and therefore provide education as cheaply as possible, at least there was a recognizable employer, with an identified source of funds and democratic accountability. More importantly still, the Union had established itself as an influence at national level and achieved, *de facto*, a right to be consulted on the major educational questions of the day.

Means of influence

At the foundation conference in 1870, 'meet-and-confer' status, or the right to be consulted (see Chapter 7), had been established as the Union's objective:

> The objects of the Union are to unite together, by means of local associations, public elementary teachers throughout the kingdom, in order to provide a machinery by means of which teachers may give expression to their opinions when occasion requires, and may also take united action in any matter affecting their interests. (NUT Founding Objects; quoted in Tropp, 1957, p. 111)

The issues listed there as requiring 'immediate attention' were revising the Code, examining the working of the new Act, the establishment of a pension scheme, greater promotion opportunities and 'the proposal to raise teaching to a profession' by means of a register. These aims are interesting for what they leave out: salaries and conditions for a start. The proposals of the Nottingham Association, which presented a straightforward trade-union shopping list, were rejected on the grounds that the Union should not concentrate so narrowly on the material

9

interests of teachers. Although two years later the Nottingham resolutions were carried in a very close vote, leading to the resignation of the Union's first General Secretary, W.F. Lawson, the Union's strategy remained based on the 1870 programme.

In pursuing its aims, the Union chose means suited to the ends. At least until 1896 it eschewed all strike action at local or national level and concentrated on exercising its powers of persuasion. At local level, this often involved direct approaches to the school boards. Certainly in the larger urban boards, London particularly, the Union rapidly gained meet-and-confer status and sometimes an element of bargaining power. Such a formal relationship was less successful elsewhere, and the Union chose instead to use its electoral weight. Until 1875 teachers could stand for election, and sometimes won. T.E. Heller, for example, the Union's General Secretary from 1873, was a member of the London School Board. Even after 1875 ex-teachers could be put forward with Union support. In any case, all candidates could be canvassed by the Union. A celebrated success came at Southampton in 1895 when, in order to redress an unfair dismissal of a member, the Union campaigned hard and ensured the election to the school board of a majority in favour of righting the wrong, including the wronged member herself (Tropp, 1957).

The Union also pressured school boards through its increasingly active legal department, which pursued over 750 'cases of difficulty' in the 1870s alone. Another option in times of dispute was to blacklist boards by trying to persuade members not to apply for posts there. This has proved surprisingly successful throughout the Union's history and was still in use in, for example, Brent in 1990.

At national level the Union focused on two centres of power. The Board of Education was an obvious target for the Union's activities and from its earliest days it submitted memoranda or took deputations to the officials and sometimes the politicians responsible for the Board. In this way it chipped away at the Revised Code, for example. At this stage the Union was not recognized – formal meet-and-confer status had not been achieved – but it clearly made some impact in any event. Formal recognition of the growing status of the Union was achieved when George Kekewich became Permanent Secretary at the Board in 1890. As he recorded later in his autobiography, 'my relations with the teachers constantly grew more cordial and intimate, and I owed to the advice of the Union officials, and the expression of opinion and the resolutions passed at Union conferences, numerous excellent suggestions' (quoted in Tropp, 1957, p. 138). The Union was increasingly involved, too, in the major commissions through which policy at national level was often developed. Yoxall, for example, sat on both the Cross Commission in 1888 and the Bryce Commission in 1895.

The second target at national level was Parliament itself. Again, there was a variety of means for influencing it. These ranged from local deputations to MPs in their constituencies, through sending memorials and other briefing material, to providing detailed information for known friends and supporters in both Houses, and to attempts to canvass all candidates at election time. From 1890 the Union kept Parliamentary Registers in which the promises made by each MP were recorded for future reference – registers which could no doubt, had they been continued, have paved the road to hell and back.

The 1877 NUT Conference resolved to seek direct teacher representation in Parliament. The first successful results of the new policy were seen in 1893 when James Yoxall, the Union's newly appointed General Secretary, and Ernest Gray, a leading member of the Union's Executive, were elected to Parliament. The Union's sensitivity about political balance was respected; Yoxall was a Liberal, Gray a Conservative, and both proved influential, particularly during the wide-ranging debate which preceded the 1902 Education Act.

By the end of the first decade of the new century, the Union had achieved a substantial degree of success using these various means of influence. For a variety of reasons, however, the Union did not rest long on the laurels of mature meet-and-confer status. Its membership had more than doubled in the 1890s and was 43,621 at the turn of the century. It continued to grow steadily, reaching 72,400 members in 1911. The restrained founding generation had been replaced by a more militant group led by Yoxall, Gray and MacNamara, who were known as the Indefatigables. The Union had therefore both growing strength and growing consciousness of its strength.

In addition, by 1910 changing social attitudes and increasing awareness of the importance of education in maintaining the competitiveness of the British economy provided teachers with important levers of power. To give but one example, the Boer War had revealed the appalling physical condition of much of British manhood, while the growing military and economic strength of Germany was increasingly apparent.

Finally, the labour and trade union movement generally in the United Kingdom, but also throughout Europe and the United States, was by 1910 revealing its might. It is not surprising to discover that the NUT, whose members largely had roots in the working class and whose pupils were predominantly of the working class, was by no means immune to this tide of militancy. In the last few years before the First World War these factors brought the education service into a period of prolonged conflict which continued until the mid-1920s.

2 Conflict: Phase One, c. 1910–1925

Early militancy

The new coherence of the education service after the 1902 Act, and in particular the fact that teachers' salaries were to be paid from the rates, provided the NUT with the opportunity to bargain directly and effectively over salaries across England and Wales. Prior to 1902 this had only been possible in the urban school boards. Furthermore, as we have seen, the growing confidence of the Union in its own strength coincided with widespread labour militancy immediately prior to the First World War. The steady increase in prices in those years led the Union to initiate its first national salaries campaign in 1913. The shortage of teachers which had resulted from the phasing out of the pupil-teacher route into the profession in the previous decade further strengthened the Union's position.

Meanwhile, the Union had already discovered that militant activity could be more effective in certain conditions than any amount of persuasion. The first major local conflict was at Portsmouth in 1896 where the school board, underestimating (indeed hoping to ignore) the strength of the local NUT, dismissed four teachers for ignoring a rule requiring attendance at 7.55 a.m. This provoked strike action because there had been growing agitation at the appalling record of the local school board in relation to both teacher salaries and investment in education. At the time, the school population was growing rapidly and pupil:teacher ratios locally (excluding heads and pupil teachers) had reached 100:1. Widespread public support from teachers all over the country enabled the teachers, who handed in their notice, to win not only the reinstatement of the four, but also new pay scales and the alteration of the 7.55 a.m. attendance rule to a more civilized 8.30 a.m. The main significance of the action in national terms, however, was that a recalcitrant school board had been forced to recognize the existence of the NUT.

There had been another successful strike at West Ham in 1907. Here a ratepayer alliance had replaced a progressive municipal socialist administration on a platform of cutting the rates. To do so, they had to cut the teachers' pay scales. The teachers, on the other hand, had the support of the remaining Labour councillors and their allies in the Labour movement. In this sense the West Ham strike was a harbinger of the conflicts in the period immediately after the First World War. The dispute had many of the features of the classic strike of the time. The Council tried to recruit blackleg labour from as far afield as Scotland, even offering a post to a person who had been bannned from teaching in the neighbouring London County Council. It insisted on its right to manage and took the view that the Union was not representative of local teachers but an interfering agent causing the conflict.

The Union, on the other hand, was well organized and had a great deal of support in the local community. As Yoxall noted at one of the 80 meetings the Union held during the three-month-long dispute,

> There were present that night in addition to so many working class parents, a number of leaders of labour organisations. The teachers who were appealing for fair play that night ... were teachers in the schools of the people and when they stood up for those schools, they stood up for the people and for the children of the people. (quoted in Lawn, 1987, p. 27)

The Union proved stronger than the Council's ruling group, which split, enabling the Union to settle. The old pay scales were to apply to those currently employed, the new to anyone appointed thereafter. The settlement itself reveals the moderation of the NUT at the time, a characteristic which sometimes divided it from its labour movement allies. As one Labour councillor pointed out at the time, 'there was hardly one trade union in ten which would settle the question on such a basis as the teachers were prepared to accept' (Lawn, 1987, p. 29). Once again, though, as in Portsmouth, the NUT had forced an aggressively anti-Union council not only to recognize its existence, but to negotiate with it and settle on predominantly its terms.

Hence, when the salaries campaign began in 1913, the Union had already demonstrated its readiness to move beyond meet-and-confer status and demand formal bargaining rights. The campaign operated on two levels. At national level the Union organized a national conference with other teacher organizations in 1913, to demand national grants to enable LEAs to raise teachers' salaries. In January 1914 a deputation took the case to the President of the Board of Education.

Meanwhile at local level the Union, through its local associations, was pressing LEAs to increase salaries. There were disputes of some kind as far apart as Glamorgan and Durham. The most bitter and protracted disputes involving strike action, however, took place in the more backward rural areas such as Herefordshire and Norfolk. In these areas, unlike the more progressive urban areas, the Union not only had to fight against some of the lowest salaries but also to establish its right to exist. In the celebrated strike at Burston (Edwards, 1974), but also to a lesser extent in Herefordshire (Lawn, 1987, p. 41), what enabled the Union to sustain its case and ultimately to triumph was the support it received from parents and the community. This was a crucial lesson for the teachers' union since, unlike the situation in industrial conflicts, in a school conflict the employer actually saves money from the moment a strike begins.

The establishment of Burnham

The Great War interrupted only temporarily the salaries campaign, and the conflict it caused. By then teachers' salaries

15

had, according to Tropp, been increased in 149 out of 321 LEAs. Furthermore, widespread public recognition of the Union's case had been achieved. Like the rest of the labour movement, the NUT firmly supported the nation at war. In fact the war and the upheavals it caused throughout Europe, far from undermining the work the Union had begun in 1913, actually strengthened its case. As the relative pay of teachers fell during the war, the NUT reopened its salaries campaign across the country. Increasingly its demands were in effect for a nationally agreed pay scale. In December 1916, for example, it called on the government to 'require Local Education Authorities' to pay 'the full union's salary scale' (Tropp, 1957, p. 210). H.A.L. Fisher, the President of the Board of Education, responded to the growing sense of crisis in time-honoured fashion and set up a Committee to inquire 'into the principles which should determine the construction of scales of salary for teachers' (*ibid.*).

His Education Act in 1918, which legislated for many long-standing Union aims including compulsory and free full-time education to the age of 14, and a strengthening of LEAs and their finances, added to the already severe teacher shortage. This gave greater weight still to the Union's demands.

Wider considerations, however, were in the minds of Fisher and his colleagues. The aftermath of war brought with it a surge of radicalism throughout the labour movement. The sweeping victories of communists and socialists in Russia, Hungary, Germany and elsewhere caused real fear among the British ruling classes. Those responsible for education had cause for greater anxiety. On the one hand, they could hardly fail to notice the leading influence of teachers in the socialist movements on the continent; on the other, they understood only too well the influence a socialist teaching profession might have on the next generation. Fisher was surprisingly frank about such fears and played on them in the Cabinet to increase the allocation of resources for education. As he wrote, for example, to the Chancellor of the Exchequer, Austen Chamberlain, in 1919:

'You will readily appreciate the influence of teachers in the country and the effect which a discontented body of 160,000 teachers may easily have in keeping alive increasing social and industrial unrest' (Lawn, 1987, p. 64). Leading figures in the labour movement reached, but with approval, similar conclusions. Fisher, however, was keen to separate teaching from the rest of the labour movement by increasing both its status and its rewards. Teachers would be given a central role in reconstructing the post-war world, but in return, 'the State will expect, and will receive from the teaching profession a measure of unstinted and zealous service on behalf of the childhood of the country' (Lawn, 1987, p. 65).

As teacher strikes swept the country in 1918 and 1919 – the most dramatic being a resounding triumph in the Rhondda valley, where the teachers' leaders were overtly socialist and embedded in the labour movement – it became clear to Fisher and his colleagues that local control of education was no longer adequate. One alternative which was seriously considered was to give teachers Civil Service status. The sense of neutrality was appealing; on the other hand, the Board would have been forced to take on a massive management role, and would have stepped directly into the firing line in cases of discontent. This would be uncomfortable to a Board more used to exercising influence from a distance and promoting a facade of evenhandedness or even neutrality when local disputes arose. In short, just as 'indirect rule' was seen by the British establishment as the best way of ruling Nigeria and the other African colonies, so it was the preferred method for administering the education service.

Once Civil Service status was ruled out, national salary scales and some of the other benefits of state employment became inevitable. Hence, the 1918 Superannuation Act was non-contributory and very rewarding for teachers. Similarly, increases in grant were made to LEAs and minimum levels of salary insisted upon. With the LEAs, through their national voice the Association of Education Committees, also demanding 'a mechanism for the settlement of the salary problem ... on a

17

national basis' (Tropp, 1957, p. 211) the way was clear for the establishment of national pay bargaining.

In September 1919, after discussions with representatives of the teachers and the LEAs, Fisher established the Standing Joint Committee on a Provisional Minimum Scale of Salaries for Teachers in Public Elementary School. If this had been set up in 1990 its title would have been abbreviated into a mouthful of letters; in the 1920s, it took its shortened name from its chairman, Lord Burnham. The Union was given representation on the Committee equal to that of the LEAs. The Committee's first recommendations for minimum salaries were overwhelmingly endorsed at a special NUT Conference before the end of 1919, and most LEAs adopted them rapidly. Over the next two years, Burnham developed a complex set of four standard scales which were applied to the various LEAs. Had the immediate post-war boom continued beyond 1921, the new status of the NUT, and the national system of collective bargaining it had demanded and won, might have been assured without further conflict. In fact, the slump and the massive cuts in public expenditure which followed – the so-called Geddes Axe – meant that the Union now had to fight to defend the settlement it had achieved.

In 1921 the NUT, together with the other teacher organizations, refused to accept either salary cuts or a 5 per cent contribution from salaries towards superannuation, though the government argued it was their patriotic duty. In February 1922 the Geddes Committee Report proposed a 5 per cent cut in teachers' salaries, raising the school entry age to 6, and a contributory pension scheme. The government decided to proceed only with the last of these, and introduced a bill to that effect. It is a measure of the lobbying power of the Union, which used newspaper advertising not for the last time, that the bill was defeated on its second reading. However, after a select committee with a loyal government majority reported in July that there had never been an implied commitment in Burnham to a non-contributory scheme, the Commons accepted the proposal for a 5 per cent contribution from teachers' salaries towards their pensions. The Union – indeed the profession – perceived this to be a major betrayal. Later in the year it was forced to accept a 'voluntary' 5 per cent cut in teachers' salaries. Nevertheless, compared to many sectors of the economy, this was a triumph. The success of the teachers' rigorous defence of their post-war settlement – for prices were falling – led the press to accuse them, in a phrase often repeated since, of 'deliberate attempts to hold the community to ransom'.

The most serious threat, however, was not the nationally agreed or imposed cuts, but the attempts by some LEAs to ignore the national settlements and hence unravel all the achievements of the NUT in the previous decade. In short, such LEAs challenged the Union's right to the status and influence that national bargaining provided. This explains the bitterness of the strikes in places like Gateshead and, above all, Lowestoft.

At Lowestoft, national pay bargaining and the existence of the Union at local level were both at stake. In an attempt to cut the rates, a local 10 per cent reduction in teachers' salaries was proposed. In spite of attempts by the authoritarian chair of the Education Committee, H.C. Adams, to imply that it was not local teachers but the interfering Union that was the cause of the conflict, the salary reduction was successfully resisted by the teachers. As in previous strikes, support from the community was the critical factor. The Union had strong links locally with the Trades and Labour Council and particularly with the Agricultural Workers. Moreover, they were able successfully to expose the fact that the blackleg 'teachers' imported by Adams were below acceptable standards. As W.G. Cove, the leader of the Rhondda strike, said at a public meeting, 'men and women who did not feel that the highest interests of the children were at stake in this struggle were not fit to teach in the Lowestoft Elementary Schools' (Lawn, 1987, p. 10)

The *coup de grâce* was the establishment by the striking teachers of strike schools, which were attended by up to 1500 pupils and which, according to visiting inspectors, were providing education more successfully than the official schools with their imported labour. So poor was the inspectors' report that it seemed likely that the Board of Education would withdraw its grant to Lowestoft. The council had no choice but to capitulate, though by all accounts the indefatigable Adams wanted to continue nevertheless.

The Lowestoft dispute marked the end of attempts by LEAs to undermine the Burnham system, though it was a number of years before all of them came into line. By the mid-1920s, then, the Union had firmly established its right to national bargaining. A period of relative stability in the relations between teachers, their employers and the government had begun, and was to last for almost forty years.

Divisions within the NUT

Before looking at the Union in this new phase of its history, it is worth examining one or two other features of the period of conflict. Firstly there were, as we have seen, divisions within the government and within many LEAs about how best to move forward after the war. Secondly there were divisions within the NUT.

Among these latter divisions, there was a strategic argument over the extent to which the Union should ally itself with the labour movement in general. The issue which posed this problem in a practical sense was whether or not the Union should affiliate to the Labour Party. There was a powerful group around leading Union radicals like W.G. Cove and Michael Conway who argued that the lessons from successful strikes, such as the Rhondda, were that the Union was most successful when it linked with other workers. For them the issue was more than tactical or strategic, however; it was ideological too. They argued that socialism in general, and the Labour Party in particular, would promote publicly funded education in a way that the Conservatives, with their close links with the private schools, would never do. Furthermore, education was one key to the liberation of working people, and it was teachers who could turn it in the lock.

The case against affiliation was put with equal vigour. The Union had valued its independence from political parties. In any case, it had to deal with whichever party happened to be in power. Instead of dividing the Union on political grounds, continued independence would maintain its unity. Its aims should be the establishment of teaching as a profession on a par with doctors and lawyers.

This last point was not necessarily at issue. Indeed, some of those who promoted affiliation argued that it could be the best way to achieve professional self-government. In the event, the issue was decided by a referendum in which two-thirds rejected the option of affiliation. Nevertheless, the Union swung substantially to the left during this period. The decision in 1919 to admit uncertificated teachers was a step away from the old craft-style unionism and towards the industrial trade union model. Moreover, militancy on the salaries issue had united support, while no doubt many teachers contributed through personal involvement and the ballot box to Labour's startling advance in the 1919 election and subsequently. Finally, the Union voted overwhelmingly in a referendum in 1919 to support the principle of equal pay for women teachers.

This decision, though a major advance in policy terms, antagonized the more patriarchal male teachers, some of whom split from the Union to form the National Association of Schoolmasters (NAS). Their particular objection was that the decision had been bounced through while many men were still away in the forces. This objection was more emotive than substantive, but provided a symbol around which they could rally those who shared their deep-seated fears.

The referendum decision also failed to satisfy the more radical women members of the Union, since the Executive, still heavily dominated by men, made it clear that they did not believe priority should be given to the equal pay issue. The establishment of a separate National Union of Women Teachers (NUWT) was the result.

There were also changes in personnel at the top of the Union, as might be expected in a period of ideological division within it. Radicals known as 'the forward movement', such as Cove and Conway, Frederick Mander and Leah Manning, became the new leaders of the NUT. Having made their names in the period of conflict, many of them came to lead it, ironically, as it metamorphosed into one of the three pillars of the educational establishment.

3 Partnership: Phase One, c. 1925–1944

By the mid-1920s, the NUT bore all the hallmarks of an established union. It had a status, influence and role in decision-making that would have amazed its first generation of leaders. The seal on its national negotiating rights was set in 1926, when the Board of Education issued a regulation which required LEAs to pay the Burnham rates unless the Board approved a variation. But its new-found status was broader and deeper than this.

At local level, the Union had a working relationship with most LEAs which enabled issues over tenure or conditions to be dealt with through formalized negotiation. Arbitrary cases of injustice had become, as a result, very much rarer. Tenure cases did not vanish, by any means, but at least there was an accepted structure for tackling them. The partnership indeed often enabled school reorganizations to be carried through with mutual co-operation, an example incidentally of the potential benefits of good industrial relations for the employer.

Meanwhile, the NUT had also established an important and increasingly close relationship with the organization which represented LEAs at national level. The Secretary of this association (the Association of Education Committees [AEC]), Sir Percival Sharp, and the Union's General Secretary from 1931, Sir Frederick Mander, worked closely together, assisting above all with the policy process which culminated in the 1944 Education Act and the newly constituted Burnham Committee of 1945. These two, in co-operation with the permanent secretary of the Board of Education, were the embodiment of the 'partnership' which characterized this phase of the Union's development, and whose destruction marked its end.

Pay, conditions and status

Tenure issues, as we have seen, had become matters which were dealt with by routine procedures. Where the Union representative and the LEA officer could not solve the problem, LEAs organized formal inquiries at which the teacher could be represented by counsel, provided normally by the Union. At national level, the Union had established a right to a hearing for teachers who believed they had been wronged by inspectors, though no statutory right existed for a teacher whose certificate had been cancelled. Meanwhile, through the establishment of a group of assistant inspectors in 1913 the government had conceded the teachers' long-standing demand for promotion to the inspectorate. This resulted in a more worthwhile and productive relationship between teachers and inspectors. A similar process occurred in relations with LEAs, many of whose officers were recruited from the ranks of the teaching profession.

In relation to pay in the 1920s and the 1930s, the NUT saw its role as defending the settlements it had achieved immediately after the Great War. The defence of the settlement in the aftermath of Geddes formed, as we have seen, an important element in the establishment of national negotiating rights.

The Depression of the early 1930s led to renewed calls for cuts in teachers' pay. The 1925 Burnham agreement – agreements in those days were built to last – was terminated by the employers' side in 1931. Then the May Committee on national expenditure recommended that 'twenty per cent is the minimum reduction which should be made' in teachers' pay, after the majority had suggested that as much as 30 per cent could have been justified.

It was a measure of the Union's strength that, as a result of its campaign against such swingeing cuts, the government initially proposed a cut of 15 per cent and then, as the protests continued, settled at 10 per cent. In the context of falling prices and massive unemployment, this cut was, once again, a relative triumph for the Union. The cut was further qualified by the government's acceptance that the cut should be seen as temporary and was 'not to be regarded as the view of the government of what should be the proper rate of remuneration of teachers under less abnormal conditions' (Tropp, 1957, p. 225). In the Burnham Committee, this imposed settlement was not accepted, and the 1925 agreement was affirmed annually until 1934 when half the cut was restored, the other half following in 1935.

While the Union's defensive strength had been demonstrated during the depths of the Depression, the later 1930s provided an opportunity for it to develop new policy. The 1925 settlement was now ten years old. It provided for four different scales which applied to different groups of LEAs. The Union's 1935 proposal to abolish the lowest two scales was met half-way, but the remaining three scales survived until 1939. By then the Union had initiated discussions with the employers over a radical revision of the salary structure, but war prevented the discussion from developing.

Nevertheless, the Union's 1938 memorandum set out a basis of the post-war settlement and is a good example of effective strategic thinking by the Union. Its basic premise was that salary level should depend not on the sex of the teacher, or on the region or type of school in which a teacher worked, but on qualifications, experience and level of responsibility. The fact that the NUT was engaged in this kind of thinking was perhaps an indication of its growing confidence. Certainly teachers' pay had increased relatively throughout the inter-war years. This, combined with growing recognition among parents, employers and government of the value of schooling, had brought about greater status for the NUT and its members. This was of critical significance as the education service was redrawn during the second half of the war.

It had made similar progress on conditions of service. The issue of extraneous duties which had exercised teachers in the earlier era had ceased to trouble them. Nevertheless, the grow-ing recognition that schools could act as agencies of other social policies added new pressures to teachers' work. School meals and their administration were one such development; there were many others, particularly in areas of social deprivation. Schools in such areas often acted as a focal point for the community, and second-hand clothes, for example, were exchanged through them. In fact, teachers themselves often initiated such activities since they normally took a serious view of their social responsi-bility. The first woman member of the NUT Executive, Mrs E. Burgwin, is known to have provided feeding for her pupils in the early 1880s. While such activities added to the burdens, and sometimes led to grumbling, there was no organized resistance to them in the inter-war years, a factor which may have assisted teachers in improving their status.

The problem of teacher unemployment, however, became a major concern in the mid-1920s and again in the early 1930s. In both cases, it was the pressure for cuts that caused the difficulty. It should be stressed that unemployment resulted not from redundancy but from newly qualified teachers who failed to secure posts. The over-supply in 1931–2 resulted from the decision of the House of Lords to reject a proposal to raise the school-leaving age to 15, after the government had prepared for it by increasing the numbers receiving training. In both periods, the NUT provided financial support for students unable to find posts, an indication of the Union's financial security and deter-mination to increase the membership on whose subscriptions it was based. In fact membership increased by some 35 per cent during the inter-war years, reaching 155, 282 in 1938.

Over the whole range of classic industrial union concerns the inter-war years can be viewed as largely successful. In relation to the wider professional aims which the Union had established in 1870 and continued to pursue, the record was less clear-cut.

Professional and educational reform

Attempts to achieve professional status on a par with lawyers or doctors did not succeed. As we have seen, in the immediate post-war period the government rejected the concept of teachers as civil servants. Within the NUT the same period saw vigorous debate about the concept of a self-governing profession. The efforts to establish a Teachers' Registration Council in the first decade of the century had convinced some Union members that attempts to achieve any General Teachers' Council would always founder on the Board of Education's determination to maintain control of teacher supply and qualification. Suspicion was exacerbated by the fact that pillars of the establishment, such as *The Times* newspaper, promoted it as a way of empha-sizing professional duty and diverting teachers from their grow-ing links with the labour movement.

The forces within the Union in favour of such a council were also powerful. Significantly, as Lawn has demonstrated, such forces came from both left and right within the Union (Lawn, 1987). Self-government, in other words, was not promoted as an alternative to effective unionism, but as a logical extension of it. Control over supply and entry qualifications would, after all, provide a powerful lever in salary negotiations.

The Teachers' Registration Council established in 1912 had no power other than 'forming and keeping a Register of such teachers as satisfy the conditions of registration established by the council' (Gosden, 1972, pp. 256–7). This toothless body remained in existence throughout the 1920s and 1930s but, since registration had no benefits, it had no impact. It never had more than half of the profession registered with it and was abolished quietly in 1949.

Through the NUT and other associations, however, teachers were able to influence the development of educational policy. The 1918 Education Act had been broadly welcomed by teachers. It ensured that at least half of education funding came from central government, scrapped fees for elementary schools and brought to an end the practice of 'half time' pupils in elementary schools. Free and compulsory education to the age of 14, a long-standing goal of the NUT, was thus assured. The Act's more ambitious proposal for continuation schools, which would have offered at least part-time education to most young people over 14, was emasculated – like so many post-Great War hopes – by the expenditure cuts of the early 1920s.

The NUT continued to campaign for the raising of the school-leaving age to 15 throughout the 1920s. Bills to that effect were introduced in 1929 and 1931, but were successfully resisted by the religious lobby, who feared the cost implications for their schools of a school-leaving age of 15. The influence of the Anglican and Catholic churches was immense, and in the present secular times can easily be underestimated. They not only successfully resisted this 'educational reform of far-reaching benefit' (*The Schoolmaster*, quoted in Tropp, 1957, p. 233), they also attempted to extend denominational teaching into provided schools and to impose religious tests for teachers applying for posts. These counter-proposals struck at the heart of the Union (its existence after all resulted from the religious compromise of 1870), which fended them off. Religious controversy did not die there; it is noticeable that the meticulous consultations undertaken by Butler in preparation for the 1944 Act were dominated by religious issues. The Butler settlement, in turn, was challenged and undermined in one of the less edifying debates during the passage of the 1988 Act.

The Union's consistency on the religious question was almost matched by its commitment during the period to secondary education for all. The demand united both a principled commitment to the importance of education and an obvious self-interest on the part of teachers in general. The NUT in particular had much to gain from an extension of the LEA-controlled secondary sector, which would enable it to recruit members there and to promote its long-standing belief in a unified teaching profession.

The Union's support for universal secondary education can be traced back at least to the debates which preceded the 1902

Education Act, but achieved much higher priority in the inter-war period, when many of its more basic trade union demands – such as national salary scales – had already been achieved. The increasing public concern with educational standards provided wider support for the Union's policy. Indeed there was a broad consensus on the issue. The Hadow Report of 1926 rec-ommended a school-leaving age of 15, and the division of schooling into primary and secondary phases at age 11. It also made the case for a secondary curriculum which was much broader than the standard grammar-school fare of the day. Secondary schools were not only to provide a general education, but were also to take account of 'the probable occupations of the pupils in commerce, industry and agriculture' (Board of Education, 1926, p. xvii).

The NUT's thinking was already substantially in advance on Hadow. Its pamphlet *The Hadow Report and After* made the case for parity of provision in all state-aided secondary schools, which it argued should be administered under 'a common Code of Regulations', but, foreshadowing debates of the 1950s and 1960s, went beyond this: 'Local Authorities should be permitted to establish post-primary schools of the multiple bias type, tak-ing all children from the age of eleven onwards' (NUT, 1928, p. 66). The Spens Report of 1938 (Board of Education, 1938), which was a powerful influence on the 1944 Act, rejected this case for 'multilateral' schools on the grounds that they would have to be too large and impersonal on the one hand, but would have sixth forms that were too small on the other. Its acceptance of the Union's case for a unified code of regulations for second-ary schools was, however, welcome.

The debate on the organization of secondary education was not settled until the 1944 Act. Indeed, it could be argued that it has never been settled, as the conflicts over comprehensive edu-cation and, more recently, city technology colleges and grant-maintained schools demonstrate. Nevertheless, in traditional British *ad hoc* style, the secondary sector grew substantially in the inter-war years. By 1939, 63.5 per cent of pupils over 11 were in some form of reorganized post-primary or secondary education, as opposed to traditional elementary schools.

Attitudes to primary education were also changing, partly as a result of the work of organized teachers, and of their higher social status. The atmosphere in schools had become less austere; teachers had increasing influence over the curriculum; and the use of corporal punishment had been reduced. The Hadow Report on Primary Education (1931) revealed the extent of the shift, in words which have become famous: 'The curriculum is to be thought of in terms of activity and experience rather than of knowledge to be acquired and facts stored' (Board of Education, 1931). As current arguments on the National Curriculum reveal, the terms of the debate have changed little in the ensuing sixty years.

The raw materials, both conceptual and social, of the 1944 Education Act were therefore in place at the outbreak of the Second World War. Only economic austerity and religious controversy had prevented the necessary reform in the 1930s. The war assisted policy-makers in cutting through the remaining thickets. On the one hand it threw into sharp relief the need for radical reform, on the other it brought about a social cohesion which had been absent during the bitter inter-war years. This provided Butler with the opportunity to bring about a widespread consensus on educational reform. What is most interesting from our point of view is the extent to which this consensus was based on the views of the largest teachers' union. In many ways the 1944 Act and the reconstituted Burnham Committee of the same year represent the high point of teacher unionism in England and Wales.

The Union's longstanding commitments to the raising of the school-leaving age and free secondary provision for all were rapidly accepted by Butler and his colleagues as essential. While the Act provided for a tripartite system of grammar, modern and technical schools, rather than a system of multilateral schools, it is clear that, as far as the Union was concerned, priority was attached to the provision of secondary education,

rather than to the form it should take. Indeed, comprehensivization remained a matter of controversy within the Union into the
1960s, and did not even at that stage have the unanimous support of members.

These are now seen as the significant elements of the Act; yet,
in the early 1940s, it was religion and the voluntary schools
which were in the eye of the storm. This controversy is directly
relevant to any attempt to assess the power of the Union in this
era. For what clearly took place was that after a conflict between
the teachers' union and two of the most powerful elements of
the establishment – the High Church and the Roman Catholic
Church – a Conservative minister legislated to the satisfaction
more of the former than of the latter. The same was not true 44
years later.

The NUT's ideal would have been the abolition of the voluntary sector. As its General Secretary – using a metaphor appropriate to the time – wrote in 1942,

> the dual system lies like a tank trap across the highway to
> educational advance. Until the administrative impotence resulting
> from this weird, outmoded yet persistent dichotomy is removed
> there will be no real educational advance, no real equality of
> opportunity for the ordinary children in the schools. (quoted in
> Tropp, 1957, p. 238)

In addition, the Union was firmly opposed to religious tests for
teachers; it also argued forcefully for the right of teachers to
provide religious instruction without interference from the
clergy. The churches – particularly the Catholic Church –
wanted religious tests to be applied in the case of appointments
to non-provided schools and greater clerical influence over
religious instruction and syllabuses.

Butler was clearly impressed by the strength of feeling among
teachers on these issues. During 1943 the so-called Revised
White Memorandum promised teachers that they would suffer
no professional disadvantage on religious grounds. It also guaranteed teachers the right to be represented in discussions at LEA

level on the agreed syllabus for religious education. This was an indication that the teachers, rather than the church ultras, had the greater influence. The 1944 Act built on this memorandum. While it required a corporate act of worship and religious education for all pupils, these had not been opposed by teachers. It also gave parents the right to withdraw children from religious instruction. It settled the voluntary issue, by offering two options to such schools. They could become voluntary-controlled, in which case the LEA would provide all costs and take responsibility for all appointments except those of teachers of religious education; or voluntary-aided, in which case the LEA would provide for the running costs but the school governors would control appointments and take responsibility for the capital costs of the buildings.

Though the voluntary sector survived, therefore, it is fair to say that the status quo had been shifted substantially in the direction of the Union. It is clear that the Union's power, and its ability to mobilize others both inside and outside Parliament, enabled the minister to resist the vested interests of the churches successfully. Butler's own tact and diplomacy were also crucial.

The Union considered the 1944 Education Act to be a great triumph. Throughout 1943 its leaders had been campaigning to inject some urgency into the reform process, a measure incidentally of their confidence that Butler would introduce legislation they could support. Once the bill became an Act in August 1944, the reaction was celebratory. As Sir Frederick Mander explained,

> The most magnificent thing in this Bill is that it removes the word 'elementary' from the nomenclature of British education. And with it goes the badge of inferiority that has so long clung to the elementary schools. Implied ... is the unification of the educational system which will be bound to be followed by unification and consolidation of the teaching profession. (quoted in Tropp, 1957, p. 243)

In short, with the Education Act of 1944 the NUT achieved a goal it had set out for over half a century before.

4 Partnership: Phase Two, c. 1944–1970

'Working relationships can still be contentious, but each party unquestioningly accepts the legitimacy and utility of the other. Trust in the motives and essential good faith of the other party is built up, leading both sides to prefer working with the established leadership group' (Kerchner and Mitchell, 1988, p. 39). This brief description of what Kerchner and Mitchell call the late generational phase encapsulates the relationships at national level between the NUT and its partners in the first twenty-five years or so after the Second World War.

Pay, conditions and status

Teachers' security of tenure had been virtually assured before the war. Indeed, the process of dealing with tenure cases changed little until the impact of local management of schools (LMS) after the 1988 Act.

Salary negotiations were conducted through the new Burnham arrangements. The 1944 Act made it a statutory requirement for LEAs to pay the rates agreed in Burnham. The main Burnham Committee covered all primary and secondary education, as the NUT had hoped. The teachers' panel therefore included not only sixteen NUT representatives but four representatives from the Association of Teachers in Technical Institutions (ATTI, which later became part of the National Association of Teachers in Further and Higher Education [NATFHE]) and six from the Joint Four secondary associations. The NUT therefore had a comfortable majority, reinforced by the fact that since the 1930s it had had a joint membership scheme with the ATTI.

Salary negotiations were naturally enough fractious affairs, particularly given the vast demands on the Exchequer in the early post-war years. The consequences of the post-war baby boom for school population meant an increasing pressure on the education budget until well into the 1960s. Demands for higher quality buildings and smaller class sizes, in addition to sheer numbers, meant that the education budget had to expand substantially as a proportion of the Gross National Product simply to maintain levels of teachers' salaries. Given steady post-war inflation on top of these pressures it is not surprising that teachers' salaries fell slightly in relative terms during the late 1940s and 1950s. The NUT's determination to maintain the general level of salary meant that inevitably the salaries of teachers with higher qualifications – graduates – fared worse than their two-year-trained colleagues. As a consequence, though the NUT demonstrably argued forcefully in Burnham on behalf of graduates, resentment grew among them. Along with other factors, this enabled other unions to recruit among graduates more successfully than the NUT in the 1960s.

The growing demand in the 1950s for women to join the profession assisted the women members of the NUT in the achievement of equal pay. As we have seen, the Union had taken a policy position in favour of equal pay for women through a referendum in 1919, but the largely male-dominated Executive never gave this policy priority during the inter-war period, when they were more concerned with resisting general salary cuts. In 1955, however, equal pay for women was achieved; to be phased in over six years. This represented a triumph for years of forceful campaigning by women within the NUT and a smaller but highly effective group in the NUWT, which had seceded from the NUT in the early 1920s. The NUWT wound itself up in 1961, its aim achieved. In practice, however, equal pay remains as elusive as ever, since women are over-represented among those groups – such as primary teachers, part-time teachers and teachers who have taken a career break – which are relatively underpaid, and less likely to have posts of responsibility.

Throughout the 1950s the NUT leadership came under increasing pressure from the membership on salaries issues. In 1955, Annual Conference censured the Executive and called on it to 'develop immediately a more militant Salaries Campaign'. In general, though, the Executive dominated the Union and delivered enough through Burnham to satisfy the membership at least until the 1960s.

The major conflict of the 1950s was over superannuation. The Government Actuary reported that the teachers' pension fund was running into debt. The government's solution was to increase the teachers' contribution from 5 per cent to 6 per cent. The NUT led a campaign of opposition and thought a victory had been won when the proposed Bill was postponed and the Minister, Florence Horsburgh, replaced. In fact her successor, David Eccles, with a newly elected and larger Commons majority, drove through the increase to 6 per cent, though he conceded that the government would cover the debt that had been accrued up until then. For the first time, the NUT took national action, calling on its members to refrain from collecting National Savings. The campaign may have assisted in assuring a better settlement in the Burnham Committee in 1956 but it failed in its main objective.

The episode is a good example of a major conflict which, while bitterly fought, did not challenge the framework within which conflict was managed. In this way it differed markedly from those which took place in the aftermath of the First World War, and again in the 1970s and 1980s, and led to the rules themselves being challenged because resolution within them proved impossible.

There were other conflicts similarly within the framework during the 1950s. Perhaps the most notable was the resistance by the NUT to an attempt by the Labour-controlled Durham LEA to impose a closed shop. Many industrial unions, of course, supported the closed shop, and the Labour authority saw their position as an act of solidarity with the organized working class. The NUT's resistance, which brought it into close co-operation with other teachers' organizations and other professional people including doctors, is indicative of both its self-image and its view that the road to salvation lay through increased status and professional conditions. In this context, the idea of a closed shop was anathema, with its denial of personal freedom.

The Union took a related position in its conflict with the Middlesex LEA. Here the authority imposed a ban on the appointment of either communist or fascist headteachers. This was perceived as an attack on individual freedom too; it was also a direct attack on the Union whose local association included a number of communists, including an ex-President of the Union. No evidence was ever produced that the communist teachers abused their positions, but the LEA was able to sustain its ban because of the general climate of opinion in the heyday of the Cold War. The fact that NUT members in Middlesex voted three to one against taking action over the issue – in stark contrast to the Durham case – is perhaps the most powerful evidence of this.

By far the most significant concerns in relation to conditions of service were the size of classes and the quality of school buildings. Though considerable capital was invested in buildings in the early post-war period, growth in the school population and the problems of neglect in the 1930s meant the demand far outstripped supply. The growing demand for teachers – just to keep pace with pupil numbers and again not always matched by supply – meant that large classes, often in excess of 40 into the 1960s, remained the rule. Teachers were also aggrieved at the growing demands of midday meals supervision. Increasingly, there were demands that such supervision should not be compulsory, but it remained so until 1967, though even after that many teachers continued to carry it out. It became one of a number of examples of schools depending on good will for their smooth running. As conflict between government and teachers intensified during the 1970s and 1980s, the area of good will, or 'voluntary duty' as it was paradoxically known, became contentious.

Professional and educational developments

The post-war era – perhaps, ironically, because of the success of the partnership between government, LEAs and organized teachers – saw no progress towards the establishment of a professional council, until the early 1960s. There were then long-winded discussions among the teacher associations, which were finally brought to a successful conclusion in 1964. Attempts to convince the Conservative Minister, Quintin Hogg, had not succeeded when Labour won the election of that year. Anthony Crosland, the incoming Minister, rejected the proposal on the grounds that there was no space in the parliamentary timetable for such legislation and that the government was in any case not in a position to cede powers such as that over entry to the profession, at a time of growing shortage.

A second approach to Crosland in 1966 was rejected for the same reasons. The influence of the civil servants, which had undermined initiatives towards professional self-government at the start of the century, remained unchanged. In any analysis of power, the strength of the civil servants in the Department of Education and Science should not be underestimated.

Their influence on the issue was only subdued by the appointment in 1968 of a minister, Edward Short, who had strong personal commitment to a General Teachers' Council, and was an NUT-sponsored MP. His commitment also enabled him to quell inter-union bickering. As a result, a joint union working party reported in 1970, proposing a teaching council that would hold a register of all qualified teachers, would take responsibility for admission and training and would control professional discipline. The working party also recommended a separate advisory body on the supply and training of teachers. It was accepted that

37

the Minister would have the power to overrule the Council if he had 'overwhelming reasons' to do so.

Again, however, an election and change of government intervened. The NUT's 1971 Conference rejected the proposal in any case. The debate reflected a conflict at the heart of teacher unionism in that era. Many members in the 1960s took the view that a General Teachers' Council would interfere with the NUT's room for manoeuvre; what mattered, they argued, was not some form of professional council, but increasing the strength of the Union. This, they argued, would be best achieved by organizational unity – a merging of the different teacher associations – rather than gestures towards professional self-government.

In fact, during the 1960s divisions among the teacher organizations seemed as wide as ever. NUT-initiated attempts to bring about unity in the early 1960s foundered on the anxiety among the smaller unions about being swallowed up. The NAS, meanwhile, gained new confidence from its admission to the Burnham forum early in the 1960s and had nothing to gain from merger with the NUT; indeed, in order to continue the rate of growth it enjoyed in the 1960s, it would have had to recruit from the NUT. As a result, it developed a narrower focus than the NUT on salaries and conditions of service and demonstrated a greater willingness in the 1960s to back this up with militant action. These divisions among teachers were both a cause and a consequence of the deepening uncertainty which began to affect the education service in general and teachers in particular, as the period of steady growth began to grind to a halt.

The growth in expenditure had indeed been little short of spectacular since the war. The number of pupils in maintained schools increased from around five million to around nine million between 1945 and 1975 (Batho, 1989). Expenditure on education as a percentage rose from 3.2 per cent in 1955 to 5.9 per cent in 1968; it should be borne in mind that this was an increased percentage of an increased Gross National Product. As a result, the issues for the unions tended to be the issues of expansion: school building, attempting to reduce class sizes, teacher supply. Meanwhile, the consensus on educational issues created by Butler – with support and assistance from the NUT – survived, largely intact, into the early 1960s.

On two aspects of education policy the consensus then began to break up. One of these was the question of comprehensive education. Some authorities – notably London and Leicestershire – had begun to develop comprehensive schools in the 1950s, but it was not until the Labour government's 1965 circular requiring LEAs to develop plans for comprehensive education that such schools became widespread. The NUT, as we have seen, had been sympathetic to the idea of 'multiple bias schools' as early as 1928. It remained so, though it also had to take account of the relatively small but disproportionately influential membership it had in grammar schools. Furthermore, throughout much of the 1950s there was a strong thread of opinion within the Union that secondary modern schools would eventually achieve parity of esteem. The NUT only moved decisively in favour of comprehensive education when 'it thought that its membership regarded it as both right and inevitable' (Kogan, 1975, p. 110). This was not until 1965, when the government was already committed to the policy. It is probably fair to say, therefore, that the NUT played only a minor role in bringing about comprehensive education, though once committed to it, it fought determinedly in its defence.

On the second education issue, the curriculum, the NUT played a more decisive role. In the immediate aftermath of the 1944 Act, it became accepted that as George Tomlinson, Minister of Education, put it, 'the Minister knows nowt about the curriculum' (Batho, 1989, p. 33). This attitude reflected not only a view that teachers knew best, but also a fear, in the shadow of totalitarianism, of government influence over what was taught. Under David Eccles, the Ministry of Education began to take a different view. A new section in the Ministry, known as the Curriculum Study Group, was established in 1962 to enable it to begin to participate in debates on the curriculum. The response from the education service was almost unanimous opposition. Sir Ronald Gould, the charismatic General Secretary of the NUT, expressed a widely held view in the Union, and the profession, that the mere existence of the Curriculum Study Group posed a threat to English liberties. As we toss and turn in the wake of the output from the National Curriculum Council (NCC), the School Examinations and Assessment Council (SEAC), and National Curriculum Working Groups, all personally appointed by the Secretary of State for Education, the response of 1962 seems over-dramatic, but that is to judge with hindsight.

Out of the furore, and under significant influence from the NUT, was born the Schools' Council, which was independent of the Ministry, but involved representatives of it along with the other partners, and which took responsibility for both curriculum and examinations (in that order of priority). It is a measure of the fear of central direction that a Conservative government motivated by a growing interest in curriculum issues established a body on which – precisely to obviate that fear – every committee was to have a teacher majority.

The NUT played an important part in both the creation and then the direction of the Schools' Council. Indeed, one writer suggests the idea of the Council may have come from Gould (Jennings, in Plaskow, 1985, p. 18). In any event, in the late 1960s and 1970s the NUT's education work centred very largely on what it could achieve through the Schools' Council. For example, it played a vital part in pressing for the reform of examinations at 16-plus, which comprehensivization made necessary. It also played an increasingly influential role in shaping examinations at 16-plus and 18-plus through teacher representatives on examination boards and their committees. On Certificate of Secondary Education (CSE) boards – the source of much of the most important curriculum development of the 1960s and 1970s – teacher unions, dominated by the NUT, played an important and often forgotten creative educational role. Even after the changes brought about through the Secondary Examinations Council, the School Examinations and Assessment Council and the rationalization of examination boards following the implementation of the General Certificate of Secondary Education (GCSE), there is still in 1991 substantial teacher representation on all the examination boards.

This, however, is to stray into the territory of the next section. By the late 1960s, a range of pressures were beginning to impact on the post-war consensus. Comprehensivization had broken the political consensus apart. The movement towards child-centred education in primary schools, which the NUT supported enthusiastically, provoked the traditionalists on the right. The raising of the school-leaving age to 16 in 1971, while a long-standing demand of the unions, brought accusations of lack of government preparation and investment.

Ultimately, it was economic imperatives that threatened the consensus. The rapid expansion could not go on for ever. It was threatened by slowing economic growth rates and the series of economic crises from 1967 on, by the perceived need to begin to limit the growth of public expenditure, and by the increasing demands of other services – health, housing and social security among them – which necessarily raised questions about expenditure on education. This change in the climate led the government and others outside of education to begin to ask questions about the value for money of education expenditure and ultimately about the accountability of the service. Among teachers and their unions it led to increasing suspicion of government and to divisions among themselves about the strategies required to defend the service they worked in. The education service was on the brink of a second period of major conflict. As Coates wrote prophetically in 1972, 'With government still trapped by low rates of economic growth and the competing demands of other public services, the scene appears set for successive confrontations with militant teachers in the 1970s' (Coates, 1972, p. 127).

5 Conflict: Phase Two, c. 1970–1990

R.D. Coates, in his important study, *Teachers' Unions and Interest Group Politics* (1972), has shown how the teachers' unions, and the NUT in particular, altered and extended their strategies as they struggled with the impact of the impending economic crisis. In particular, he explains convincingly the entry of the NUT into the Trades Union Congress (TUC) in 1970 as a response to the realization that restrictions on teachers' salaries were a result of national economic policy – particularly implicit or explicit public sector pay restraint – on which the Union outside the TUC had little or no impact. It was nevertheless a divisive issue within the NUT, and among teachers. The NAS and the ATTI had already joined in the late 1960s. The other teacher associations still remain outside it. In the NUT itself a referendum in 1968 had actually voted against entry on a low turnout and a slender majority, but Conference in 1969 overturned this decision.

Nevertheless, it is possible to see the early 1970s as the Indian summer of the partnership era. In its opposition to the Conservative government's 1971 Industrial Relations Act, the NUT was able to demonstrate its new-found links with the broader labour movement. The major national strike campaign of 1969, when teachers, with others, had broken the Labour government's prices and incomes policy, had shown the strength of the teachers' unions. The campaign involved the NUT in national strike action for the first time. It influenced salary negotiations in the early 1970s and in a sense, as Seifert has pointed out, 'the real reward' for 1969 was the Houghton Committee's

1974 recommendation, which raised teachers' salaries dramatically and even now remains the baseline for union salary claims (Seifert, 1987, p. 111).

The early 1970s also saw the NUT's influence over educational developments at its zenith. The Schools' Council was the major national influence on the curriculum, and its dominant figures were from the teacher unions. As Maurice Plaskow explains, 'the NUT group was powerful: it was large and articulate, well serviced by its officers, so that the representatives came to meetings fully briefed' (Plaskow, 1985, p. 3); but he points out that representatives of other unions too contributed powerfully: 'If teachers had the major influence in Council policy during the 1970s it was because they brought greater commitment to its work, and the groups did not appear to object strongly to the general direction' (*ibid.*). The general direction is neatly summarized by Jean Rudduck: ' "No curriculum development without teacher development" was our slogan' (Rudduck, in Plaskow, 1985, p. 148).

In spite of the growing economic pressures, the government in the early 1970s appeared to accept teacher influence in this area: 'it is vital that those who train teachers should be familiar with the work of the Schools' Council', argued Margaret Thatcher in 1973 (quoted in Plaskow, 1985, p. 8). Furthermore, in her major White Paper, *A Framework for Expansion*, the curriculum was not mentioned at all (DES, 1972). More importantly still, from the teachers' point of view, the White Paper envisaged continuing expansion: 'The last ten years have seen a major expansion of the education service. The next ten will see expansion continue – as it must if education is to make its full contribution to the vitality of our society and our economy' (DES, 1972).

The international oil crisis of the following year, however, revealed the full extent of the weakness of the British economy, which, as we have seen, had already begun to affect the relations between government and teacher unions. For this reason, the Houghton award of 1974 was not followed, as might have been expected, by a long period of stability, but instead by a relationship of growing acrimony with governments of both major political parties. The conflict ceased to be one within the partnership framework and became, particularly after Thatcher's election in 1979, one which sought to alter, in a fundamental way, the relations between teachers, their employers and the government. It also resulted in divisions within each of those groups about the best way forward: it was therefore a conflict affecting the education service root and branch, from which, it would be fair to say, it has not yet fully emerged.

The assault on the power of teacher unions in education has four separate strands: the government's perceived need to control public expenditure, the tendency towards centralization, demands for accountability, and the direct assault on trade unions and their involvement in national level policy-making. Clearly the four strands form, at any rate in the mid- and late 1980s, part of a coherent government strategy. Though in what follows they are separated for analytical purposes, it is the intention to reveal also the relationship between them.

The control of public expenditure

Governments of both parties have made stringent attempts to control public expenditure since the mid-1970s. An important aspect of this – and one they have found incorrigibly difficult – has been the control of local government's expenditure. Since teachers' salaries form a substantial proportion of expenditure at local level, it is not surprising that they have come under severe pressure during that time. Government influence over teachers' pay has been extended in three ways; firstly by increasing government influence in the Burnham forum, secondly by cutting central government support to local government, and thirdly by restricting the ability of local government to raise taxes.

As far back as 1961, the Minister of Education had intervened in the Burnham process to try to implement the government's 'pay pause'. From then on, government sought a more direct influence. This was achieved with the 1965 Remuneration of Teachers Act which, along with the Concordat with the LEAs, gave the government direct representation on Burnham, a right of veto over the global sum of any award, and a weighted vote over its distribution. It also gave the Minister the right to vary the membership of the Burnham Committee.

These powers were used during the 1980s to restrict the sum available for negotiation and in 1985 to reduce the influence of the NUT on the Burnham Committee by removing its overall majority. However, these powers were essentially negative. Their effect was to give the government the power to create deadlock rather than settlement. It was this that motivated the impatient Kenneth Baker, Secretary of State for Education from 1986 to 1989, to sweep away the whole Burnham framework in the 1987 Teachers' Pay and Conditions Act, which gave him the power to impose a settlement and a contract of employment after taking advice from a government-appointed advisory committee. This decision to abolish teachers' right to negotiate was, at least in part, a result of the government's growing frustration at its inability to control public expenditure. Its dubious consequences in educational terms on morale, recruitment and retention were not taken into account.

Other attempts to control expenditure had proved similarly frustrating. Central government support was progressively cut from 1976 onwards. As a percentage of local government expenditure, central government support fell from 71 per cent in 1976–7 to 47.5 per cent in 1986–7. Over a decade this was, as Gordon Batho has commented, 'a stupendous reduction' (Batho, 1989, p. 50). Local government, however, proved remarkably resistant to passing on the cuts in the form of reduced levels of service, partly of course as a result of the strength of teachers' and other public sector unions. Their response to such cuts was to increase the rates.

This drove the Conservative government, which had ideological monetarist grounds as well as pragmatic grounds for restricting public expenditure, to introduce a series of measures to restrict local government's powers to raise finance. Supplementary rates were outlawed, penalties for spending over government proposed levels were introduced and then central government power to cap rate levels was implemented. A brief era of 'creative accountancy' followed, in which councils found loopholes in the extraordinarily complex legislation, which even government ministers had ceased to understand. The culmination of these reforms was the implementation in 1990 of the poll tax. Paradoxically, while the poll tax proved successful in restricting local government expenditure – the year after its implementation saw cuts in many authorities – it was disastrous in all other respects. Once its most ardent advocate, Margaret Thatcher, had been removed, the government set out first to review it and then to bury it altogether. Sisyphus, now in the form of Michael Heseltine, began to push the rock up the hill once again. Whatever form the new local or council tax takes, one aspect is certain: the proportion of local government services paid for directly by central government will be higher than ever. The answer to the conundrum which puzzled Conservative ministers throughout the 1980s turns out to be a revised version of 'he who pays the piper calls the tune'. As a result, there is widespread discussion about whether local government should have a significant role in education at all.

The consequences of these restraints in the 1980s have not been restricted to reductions in teachers' pay. There is no doubt that the quality of educational buildings – one-third of schools had leaking roofs in 1987 – has become a matter of major concern, as has the level of provision of books and equipment. By 1985, Her Majesty's Inspectorate (HMI) were reporting that poor levels of material provision were detrimentally affecting educational standards. As Tim Brighouse pointed out in a speech at the 1990 NUT National Education Conference, a generation ago school buildings, in inner cities at least, were often of high quality and had better provision than people's private circumstances allowed. This is now rarely the case.

The Enquiry into Discipline in Schools – headed by Lord Elton, a former Conservative minister – identified poor buildings as a factor in declining standards of discipline (DES and Welsh Office, 1989). There is no doubt too that it contributes to the teacher shortage. The solution to the problem, as the NUT and some LEAs have repeatedly pointed out, requires massive investment. The encouragement by government of parental contributions to schools and of other forms of sponsorship, apart from its obvious iniquity, is no solution.

The teachers' response to the restrictions on expenditure have gone far beyond pointing out the detrimental consequences in educational terms. The teacher unions were closely involved in protecting their members during the reorganization which resulted from the falling school rolls of the late 1970s and the 1980s. While it could be argued that one consequence of this work has been the retention of surplus places in the system, which is a drain on expenditure, the unions were remarkably successful in their central aim of protecting their members' jobs. There were no compulsory redundancies during the 1970s and 1980s as a result of reorganization. The significance of this is brought into sharp relief when the devastation of other sectors of the economy, such as mining, shipbuilding and printing, during the same period is considered.

The NUT – like some other teacher organizations – also resisted the pressure on salaries and education expenditure through what became almost endemic action. This sometimes took the form of withdrawal of good will and sometimes of coordinated strike action across the country. It reached a peak in the pay dispute of the mid-1980s, which is examined in detail later in the chapter. One result of it, as we have seen, was the abolition of teachers' negotiating rights. Another was a growing dissatisfaction among parents with education and, to some extent, with teachers and their unions. Nevertheless, it should be recognized that the pay settlement imposed by Kenneth Baker in 1987, while less satisfactory than the deal the unions and the employers had reached at Nottingham in late 1986, was a major improvement on previous government offers. The conflict of the mid-1980s over teachers' salaries was therefore by no means an unqualified defeat for the teachers.

Increasing central control

The increasingly important role central government played in deciding teachers' salaries – up to the point, indeed, where it became a diktat – has already been explained. This tendency towards centralization, however, extended to other areas of education policy, including particularly the curriculum, teacher education and the nature of secondary school provision. The earliest attempt of post-war government to intervene in the curriculum, the 1962 Curriculum Study Group, was transformed, as we have seen, into the Schools' Council, which became a focus for partnership between teachers, local government and the central government, with the teacher element in the ascendancy.

Further moves towards direct government influence on the curriculum were left until the mid-1970s. By then there were two full-blown controversies in the curriculum policy area: one between traditionalists and proponents of child-centred education over the primary curriculum, and another, related, debate over comprehensive education and its curriculum and assessment implications. The radical right was asserting itself on the side of tradition, elitism and national heritage through the vituperative Black Papers (Cox and Dyson, 1971). The extremes of child-centredness seen and publicized at William Tyndale School played into their hands (ILEA, 1976). Meanwhile, the economic crisis of the mid-1970s led employers and government to question whether the education service was adequately preparing the nation's young for adult life and work.

It was in this context that James Callaghan launched what he called 'the Great Debate' about education in 1976. He argued in an influential speech at Ruskin College: 'I am concerned on my journeys to find complaints from industry, that new recruits from the schools do not have the basic tools to do the job that is required. ... There is unease about the new informal methods' (quoted in NUT, 1990a, p. 7). In the debate that followed, the Department of Education and Science (DES) and HMI, though with differing emphases, called for greater central direction. The 1977 Green Paper, for example, explained that: 'The Secretaries of State will therefore seek to establish a broad agreement with their partners in the education service on a framework for the curriculum' (DES, 1977). By 1980, the view had become firmer: 'The Secretaries of State believe that they should give a lead in the process of reaching a national consensus on a desirable framework for the curriculum' (DES and Welsh Office, 1980).

Similar positions were taken in DES and HMI documents during the early 1980s. The first direct curriculum intervention, however, was the Technical and Vocational Education Initiative, announced in 1982. The proposal channelled funds through the Manpower Services Commission rather than the DES, with the intention of supporting curriculum projects for 14–18-year-olds to improve preparation for the world of work. It was unwelcome, on the whole, to the NUT, though in time the Union was able to exert considerable influence on the project because its National Steering Group included the General Secretary, Fred Jarvis, as a representative of the TUC. Indeed, it proved eventually to be a fine example of how teachers could transform a project designed for narrow purposes into a major curriculum development success.

The climate of curriculum debate, however, had been poisoned by the announcement six months earlier that the Schools' Council was to be wound up. Sir Keith Joseph, the Secretary of State for Education, ignored the Trenaman Report (DES, 1981), which he had asked for, and proposed instead of the Schools' Council two separate bodies, the Secondary Examination Council (SEC) and the Schools Curriculum Development Committee (SCDC). In both cases, their membership was appointed entirely by the Secretary of State. Significantly, the SCDC was set up later with a smaller budget and less status. The assessment cart was put back in front of the curriculum horse.

The centripetal tendency of government policy continued through the *Better Schools* White Paper (DES and Welsh Office, 1985) and the 1986 Education Act, which not only required each LEA to produce a statement of its curricular aims, but also 'banned' politically biased teaching. Throughout the period, the government was operating in a climate of vitriolic attack against publicly provided education, developed by right-wing pamphleteers such as Stuart Sexton, and whipped up by its supporters in the popular press. It was argued – without foundation and evidence – that teachers' concern with equal opportunities, anti-racism and anti-sexism was undermining standards or was even part of a Marxist-inspired plot. It is no coincidence that this reached its height at the time the salaries dispute was at its most bitter. In any case, it paved the way for the National Curriculum proposals of the 1988 Education Reform Act, which took the centralization of the curriculum to levels not seen since payment by results disappeared in the 1890s. As 1990 progressed, the government itself seemed to have taken fright at the extent of its control. At Easter of that year, Thatcher expressed her anxiety at the level of detailed prescription, and later in the year its extent in geography and history was reduced. Nevertheless, it remains excessive and would have seemed unthinkable only a few years ago.

Whatever the result of the continuing debate, the machinery established by the 1988 Act leaves curriculum and assessment firmly in the hands of the Secretary of State and the two bodies which he or she appoints, the NCC and the SEAC. It is a measure of how far centralization has gone that the teacher unions considered it a victory, in June 1990, when the NCC agreed to appoint 'a teacher' to those of its committees on which there were none. In the summer of 1991 these committees were in any case wound up. At the same time the removal in quick succession of Duncan Graham and Philip Halsey, who headed the NCC and SEAC respectively, and their replacement by close political allies of the Conservative right, was a sharp reminder of the extent to which direct political control of the curriculum has developed.

While teachers have been systematically excluded from curriculum and assessment policy decisions during the 1980s, the government has also increased its control over teacher education. Since 1944, and even earlier, teacher training and education had been a government responsibility. Nevertheless, by 1972, pressure from the NUT and others had successfully established a commitment to the 'all-graduate profession'. The integration of initial teacher training with the rest of higher education represented the achievement of a long-standing goal for the NUT. The later 1970s were dominated, however, by college closures as training capacity was dramatically reduced (from 120,000 in 1972 to 55,000 in 1981). In the 1980s, central government began to take control of course content. The government-appointed Council for the Accreditation of Teacher Education (CATE), set up in 1984, set criteria which all courses had to meet. It was greeted with howls of protest from teachers and teacher educators. Though by 1988 it had won grudging support from the profession, it nevertheless represented a new stage of centralization. A new government circular introduced in 1989 took this a stage further, linking the CATE criteria to the National Curriculum and other recent reforms.

Meanwhile, the Advisory Committee for the Supply and Education of Teachers (ACSET), which was representative of the teacher organizations and the LEAs, was stood down in 1985 and never recalled. Its proposals for reforming in-service education were, however, adapted to give the government greater influence and implemented in 1987. Each year since then, in spite of the almost unanimous opposition from the profession, the extent of in-service education funding devoted to central government priorities has increased steadily. In 1990, local priorities as such were scrapped altogether. The use of in-service training funds and of other specific central government grants to implement the government agenda for educational change has been a feature of the 1980s which is likely to be maintained in the 1990s. Union demands for a representative national body to discuss priorities for such expenditure have gone unheeded, although precisely such a body was recommended by the Conservative-controlled Commons Select Committee on Education in May 1990. This may be a sign of growing realization that central domination has severe costs in educational terms.

By 1991, the comprehensive system of secondary education was also severely threatened by central government intervention. The NUT, as has been seen, had taken a firm policy position in favour of comprehensive education in the mid-1960s. It has maintained that view since then, and has defended the comprehensive system against the various attacks made on it in the intervening period. It is worth pointing out, however, that comprehensive education only became as widespread as it did because in 1976 the government legislated to enable it to require LEAs to prepare plans for comprehensive reorganization. It is also worth remembering that the evidence clearly shows that the move towards comprehensive education was popular at the time. In spite of this, some die-hard LEAs managed to stagger through with grammar schools until the 1980 Act withdrew the comprehensive requirement.

Throughout most of the 1980s, the integrity of the comprehensive system survived intact. At LEA level, after all, it had broad cross-party support. The 1988 Education Reform Act, however, was designed in part to undermine it. It did this through delegation of financial control to school level and the implementation of market forces on the one hand, and through increased central control on the other. Grant-maintained status, or opting out, while presented as giving freedom to schools, actually results in a sector of education which is directly dependent on the DES and clearly receiving favoured financial treatment. The city technology college (CTC) programme is even more blatantly interventionist in both policy and financial terms. It has been given such priority that over £120 million of central government funds have been devoted to it at a time of financial stringency. In spite of this, the programme appears to have spluttered to a halt, owing to a lack of enthusiasm for it among industrialists.

The role of central government has therefore extended far beyond what might have been imagined at the start of the decade. The UK now has one of the most centralized education systems in the western world. The NUT's response to this process has been a mixed one. In the early 1980s, it took a purely defensive role in which the Union argued in defence of the status quo. It refused, for example, to have formal contact with the SCDC in its early days because it was government appointed rather than representative. In 1985 the motion it proposed at the TUC Conference condemned growing central control of the curriculum and other aspects of policy. Nevertheless, the defensive response was already becoming more pragmatic. The proposals it made for the reform of in-service training, for example, favoured increased DES influence because only in this way could ineffective LEAs be brought into line. Later in the decade, the Union supported proposals for a national system of teacher appraisal for the same reasons, though in both cases it argued for nationally representative bodies to oversee the policy. It had, of course, supported national-level pay negotiations since before the First World War, and continued to do so. It was not simply that some LEAs would not implement policy unless it was nationally imposed; it was also that government would only finance it if it was convinced it was worth prioritizing at national level. Records of achievement, which were widely supported in the service and of proven educational merit, were in decline by 1990 because the government was only prepared to support them in word, not in deed. The records of achievement introduced by government were little more than extended reports and barely deserve the name.

Nevertheless, the NUT remained implacably opposed to the extent to which, by the end of the 1980s, the government influenced the nature of teachers' work. The Union was no longer arguing simply for teachers' rights to control the curriculum, as it had in the 1960s and 1970s; instead, it emphasized the importance of an element of flexibility and professional freedom if teachers were to be motivated and hence the quality of education enhanced. In arguing this, ironically, it was able to draw on modern management theory, which promoted collaborative models of working, delegation and management on the basis of trust. Teacher control of the curriculum had, however, been ceded. As the NUT argued in *A Strategy for the Curriculum*, 'The old model [of the curriculum] fails to recognise the legitimate interests of parents, pupils, the community and, indeed central government in what pupils learn' (NUT, 1990a, p. 18). The accountability of teachers to those outside the profession had been explicitly recognized.

The call for accountability

Implicit in the Great Debate was the view that employers, parents, government and the community had rights to influence what took place in schools. The post-war assumptions that a steady increase in expenditure and provision would be matched by increasing satisfaction with education had fallen apart. It was inevitable, particularly once control of public expenditure became a central political objective, that questions would be asked about how money was being spent. Furthermore, as the political consensus on education broke up, and education policy became increasingly contested, different interests were bound to attempt to influence the policy process. Some of these interests, such as 'employers' and 'parents', were exploited by governments, particularly the Thatcher government, in support of policies to which the governments were ideologically committed. 'Parents', for example, were said to favour 'choice' though in opinion polls most expressed themselves satisfied with their local school.

Growing concern with the question of accountability took differing and sometimes contradictory forms. The Taylor Committee, established by the Labour government in 1976 to look at school government, recommended 'a new partnership' at school level, with teachers, parents and LEAs to be equally represented on governing bodies. The 1980 and 1986 Acts in large part implemented its recommendations, though the extent of teacher representation was proportionately cut. It is remarkable that what was effectively employee representation on the board survived at all given the climate during the salaries dispute. At the time of Taylor, the NUT opposed it on the grounds that it threatened professional control, but by 1986 the Union was arguing for the Taylor proposals in place of the 1986 Act.

The Union also opposed publication of public examination results and of HMI reports in the early 1980s, but once implemented, neither of these changes had a significant impact, except in cases of particularly shocking HMI reports such as that on Hackney Free and Parochial School early in 1990 (DES, 1990a). It could, in any case, be argued that cases of such chronic neglect are indeed matters of public concern. The issue then becomes how best to rebuild the school's effectiveness. In short, the NUT's automatic opposition in the early 1980s to a wider accountability, even where it had a legitimacy in a democratic society, neither protected the profession nor promoted improved educational quality.

Under Sir Keith Joseph, Secretary of State for Education from 1981 to 1986, the government sought to take accountability beyond the relatively gentle measures of 1980 and 1981. The 1983 White Paper, *Teaching Quality* (DES, 1983), called for a punitive form of teacher appraisal linked directly to reward and dismissal. These proposals gained support in sections of the popular press, and among some LEAs. The NUT, however, was able to convince Keith Joseph that appraisal could either improve quality or allocate reward and punishment, but not both. In November 1985, Sir Keith publicly accepted that what he sought was appraisal for development, not accountability.

By then, he had already flirted with, and retreated from, a more radical form of accountability; accountability to the market, through the concept of vouchers. The idea, beloved among the right-wing think-tanks, was that parents should be given an educational voucher to pay part or all of the cost of whatever school, private or state, they chose for their children.

In this way, schools would be forced to provide what parents wanted, or go under. This idea went far beyond the mild concept of parent governors in the 1980 Act, or annual reports to parents as in the 1986 Act. Officials convinced Sir Keith that the idea of vouchers was unworkable – not least because of the huge subsidy it would provide to the private sector – but the idea of accountability to the market, which after all was being systematically applied to publicly owned industry through privatization, remained attractive in Conservative circles.

Indeed, the proposals put to the electorate during the 1987 election campaign by Kenneth Baker, who had replaced Sir Keith a year earlier, amounted to an alternative way of imposing market accountability. Formula funding, delegated budgets and open enrolment became elements in the 1988 Education Reform Act, and are currently being implemented. Without a doubt they are, in their own terms, beginning to work.

The NUT, like the overwhelming majority of the education profession, opposed the reform root and branch. It argued that market forces would lead to inequality and elitism and would threaten its members' security of tenure. It would also undermine the ability of LEAs to plan. The accuracy of these predictions is increasingly borne out by experience. In spite of the strength of opposition, the government, with its overwhelming Commons majority, was able to put the market model in place. The Union's historic resistance to all forms of accountability and the strains on relations between teachers and parents resulting from the action of the mid-1980s undoubtedly contributed to the government's success. Nevertheless, the government's claim that it would raise standards – as opposed to the Union's that it would reduce them for the majority – remains very much in doubt. The consequences for the morale of teachers, a factor contributing to teacher shortage, which is recognized by all but the government as extremely serious, are not in doubt.

As the NUT begins to map out a strategy for the 1990s, it may take a crumb of comfort if its prediction that government reforms would lower standards proves correct. More importantly, it has developed a more sophisticated position on accountability. While remaining implacably opposed to market accountability, it has begun to argue for a form of accountability likely to be both more popular with parents, and more beneficial educationally.

> Parents and others ought to be informed about the success of the school their child attends, but the publication of raw test results serves political, not educational, purposes and is unlikely to affect achievement. In its place there needs to be discussion at national level centred on what an effective school is and how its effectiveness can be evaluated. This process should lead to parents and others receiving a much more accurate picture of schools than published test results can ever provide. (NUT, 1990a, p. 19)

The end of partnership

The Conservative government elected in 1979 made no secret of its intention to reduce the influence of trade unions throughout British society. The steps by which they did so – assisted by economic crisis and unemployment – need not be traced here. The consequences of the government's attitude in the education sector were, however, an important factor in the conflict of the 1980s.

Much of the NUT's influence in the post-War period was, as we have seen, exerted through the close relations it had developed from the 1920s onwards with its 'partners', the LEAs and the DES. This manifested itself in the exhaustive consultations which preceded proposed policy changes, in various consultative forums, such as ACSET and the Schools' Council, and in the often close personal relations between officials of the various organizations. Ronald Gould (General Secretary of the NUT), William Alexander (Secretary to the Association of Education Committees) and officials of the DES were said to be the basis of policy development in the 1960s. Tropp makes a similar claim for the 'friendly and conspiratorial' triumvirate of Sir Percival Sharp (AEC), Sir Maurice Holmes (Board of Education) and Sir

Frederick Mander (NUT in the 1930s and 1940s) (Tropp, 1957). The claims may be exaggerated but they illustrate the strength of the partnership, which depended not only on a recognition of the unions as the voice of teachers, but also on a desire to draw on their expertise, or 'technical power', to use Manzer's term (Manzer, 1970). As Coates argues, 'the growing closeness of the relationship between the associations and the Department was [in part] a product of the Department's own need for advice, acquiescence and approval as the scale of its activity increased' (Coates, 1972, p. 119).

The growing rancour of the 1960s and 1970s had already put partnership under pressure; government policy in the 1980s tore it asunder. We have already seen how the Schools' Council was abolished, ACSET stood down and Burnham replaced. The idea of a right to be represented in national-level policy discussions had gone. Indeed, if Maurice Kogan's view of the NUT as a legitimized interest group had validity in 1975, one might have questioned it by 1988. It is true that the DES was still willing in general to receive deputations, but the gulf between the sides was often such as to restrict discussion to an exchange of views. As Maclure has pointed out, the Conservative government had made a conscious decision to develop policy outside the educational establishment, which it viewed as woolly and self-interested (Maclure, 1989). Teacher unions as both part of the educational establishment and trade unions were doubly excluded. Indeed, when Alan Howarth, a junior education minister, spoke at an NUT conference on teacher appraisal in January 1990, it was the first time for four years that such an event had occurred.

The contrast between Kenneth Baker's attitude to the NUT during the debates on the 1988 Act and Butler's forty-odd years previously is dramatic. The result has been not only controversy, and profound division, but also a loss of the ability of central government to draw effectively on the technical power of the unions. The avowed intent of John MacGregor, Secretary of State for Education from July 1989 to October 1990, to listen to the teachers indicated a recognition of the damage this had done, but under Kenneth Clarke there has been a return to the megaphone approach.

Meanwhile, the trade union legislation of the decade applied as forcefully to the teacher unions as to others. One of the main reasons the NUT had joined the TUC in 1970 was, as Coates has convincingly shown, to gain access to the levers of national economic policy. Yet since 1979, precisely in that capacity the TUC's influence has been emaciated. Despite this, the value of membership has never been seriously questioned; it has enabled the NUT to work with other unions, particularly public sector ones, and to break down the distance there had been between the NUT and its industrial counterparts in the past. It has also enabled it to participate in the rethinking of trade unionism that began to take place in the late 1980s.

The pay dispute of the mid-1980s

The earlier part of this chapter has examined the elements which combined to form the government's attack on the teaching profession. Throughout those sections the events of the 1970s and 1980s have been examined to illustrate the argument.

In this section the aim is to examine the dispute at the apex of the crisis, a dispute which was the most serious and sustained period of industrial conflict in the history of this country's education service. An examination of the teachers' dispute of 1984–7 provides, therefore, an instructive insight into the themes of this chapter. It also reveals fascinating glimpses of the pressures under which a major union operates, pressures which very often come not only from outside, but also from within. In the case of the teachers' dispute, its byzantine complexity can only be understood in the context on the one hand of a powerful government on the offensive, and on the other of inter- and intra-union rivalry, which constantly hampered the teachers' efforts.

Since the dispute and its consequences remain one of the strongest influences on current educational politics, it is surprising that so little has been written about it. The chief source remains R.V. Seifert's work, which is based on an extensive examination of the sources. His attempt to bring these together into a detailed narrative has been an essential service to educational history. However, the book also has severe flaws. Published as it was in 1987, it was obviously unable to look back on the dispute with the sense of perspective which has now become essential. More seriously still, it is prone to making ill-judged and unsustained assertions. To take but one example, Seifert argues that, 'After the June 1983 general election teachers, and their trade union representatives, recognised the inevitable consequences for them of the dominance of Mrs Thatcher's conservatism' (Seifert, 1987, p. 179). The inevitable consequences, he alleges, were the replacement of partnership by cuts, centralization and privatization. As we have seen there were elements of all of these running back to 1979, yet the assumption of an unbridgeable gulf between teachers and the government ignores the fact that in 1983 a larger proportion of teachers voted Conservative than for any other party.

Later on he describes the LEAs' statement that they could 'only pay for what they can afford' as 'an astonishingly overstated and politically determined outburst' (Seifert, 1987, p. 184). Aside from the fact that it is the role of LEAs to determine things politically – it is after all the reason for having local democracy – their statement is guilty not of being astonishing but of being platitudinous. Seifert's analysis and judgement are therefore highly questionable. His painstaking research, by contrast, provides the essential background for any study of the 1980s pay dispute, including this one.

From 1984 onwards both the complexity and the bitterness of the dispute over teachers' pay and conditions increased. The dispute's complexity resulted from the fact that it involved the question not just of pay, but also of conditions and the mechanisms for negotiating both pay and conditions (the Burnham Committee for pay, and the Council of Local Education Authorities/School Teachers [CLEA/ST] for conditions). It also needs to be borne in mind that, by the mid-1980s, teachers' salaries had returned almost to pre-Houghton levels in relative terms. This issue of comparability with other non-manual workers helps to explain the determination of many classroom teachers to continue in dispute for so long.

In part the bitterness was caused by determination on both sides, and in particular by the intransigence of a government firmly committed, as we have seen, to the tight control of public expenditure. However, it was the divisions within each side that exacerbated it. On the employers' side there was a constantly rumbling split between the Labour and Conservative representatives and between the metropolitan authorities and the county councils. On the teachers' side there was rarely unanimity and often division. Where the splits occurred between and within unions they changed in kaleidoscopic fashion. Such divisions were often historic, as Rene Saran reveals in her study of the politics of Burnham (Saran, 1985); the tension of the dispute heightened them and brought them to the surface.

At the outset of the dispute in 1984, while the teachers were united on a pay claim of 7.5 per cent, they were divided over whether to link negotiation over conditions with those over salaries. The NUT was resolutely opposed to any such linkage: the National Association of Schoolmasters/Union of Women Teachers (NASUWT), on the other hand, was prepared to trade one for the other. It was academic in any case, since the employers' offers of 3.0 per cent and then 4.5 per cent were unacceptable to all the teacher organizations. When the teachers' panel, which at that stage had an NUT majority, called for arbitration the employers refused.

Their decision led to a withdrawal of good will by the NUT. This involved non-co-operation with those activities which teachers carried out – such as lunchtime supervision – but which were not considered to be contractual obligations. At the same time teachers were encouraged to lobby local councillors.

On 9 May 1984, the NUT called a one-day national strike. Later in the month in various local authorities over 20,000 NUT members were involved in three-day strike action. It was during this phase that the NUT and the NASUWT first began to co-ordinate their action after a meeting held under the TUC umbrella. Throughout the dispute the two organizations found it easier to co-ordinate action than to unite on their negotiating strategy.

As a result of this period of sustained action, the employers conceded the teachers' demand for arbitration on 22 June 1984. The result of arbitration was, however, a bitter blow to the teachers' side, resulting as it did in an award of 5.1 per cent – only fractionally above the employers' offer rejected a few months earlier. As a consequence, the NUT never again had faith in the arbitration process under the Burnham system.

The 1985 claim submitted by the teachers was drawn up in this context. Proposed by the NUT and put through the teachers' panel by their majority, it was for a flat-rate increase of £1200, linked to progress on the pay structure. The claim had been controversial within the NUT at its Easter Conference, and was opposed by the headteacher unions and the Assistant Masters and Mistresses Association (AMMA). It was in any case flatly rejected by the employers and, with the unions opposed this time to the process of arbitration, deadlock ensued once more.

Running parallel to the conflict over pay was a long-winded series of discussions over how to reform the pay structure, which in turn was linked by the employers and some unions to revised conditions of service and an end to the tradition, which stretched back to the creation of Burnham in 1919, of negotiating pay and conditions separately. The issues in dispute included the government's desire to see pay linked to performance appraisal, and the differing views of the protagonists on the number of posts of responsibility and the extent of the salary bill which should be spent on them. These issues remained unresolved when the NUT pulled out of the structure talks towards the end of 1984.

It is also important to bear in mind that the dispute over pay took place against a backdrop of education cuts affecting books, equipment and school buildings as well as teachers' pay. Furthermore, there was a high level of tension between the trade union movement in general and the government as a result both of the exclusion of unions from GCHQ in 1984 and also the miners' strike, which lasted well into 1985. Adding to the climate of chaos and despondency was growing conflict, as we have seen, between the local authorities and central government over expenditure levels and particularly the application of rate-capping.

It was therefore no surprise when the Burnham talks collapsed in February 1985. Strike action and the withdrawal of good will by the major teachers' unions followed immediately. What had once been a very rare occurrence had by now – as a result of the depth of division – become part of the culture.

During the months that followed, the NUT held a series of ballots on various action proposals, all of which received overwhelming endorsement. In the West Midlands over 150,000 pupil days were lost to strikes in March 1985. The action rolled inexorably into the summer term as the local authority employers found their room for manoeuvre tightly constricted by Sir Keith Joseph, the Secretary of State for Education.

Meanwhile, the NUT – in a process to some extent mirrored in other teacher organizations – led by its members, became increasingly militant and therefore less likely to accept compromise. At the 1985 Conference, the NUT decided to ballot on an extension of non-strike action. Sanctions agreed by Conference and later endorsed in a ballot included a refusal to complete records and reports out of school time or to be involved in curriculum innovation. Both decisions, while understandable in the context of the highly charged atmosphere of a conference during a pay dispute, were to cause major problems in the longer term. The decision on reports damaged relations with parents. The decision on involvement in innovation was followed by a boycott of training for the new GCSE examination. The government, however, refused to change the implementation timetable. At the last minute, therefore, the union reversed its position, leaving neither moderates nor militants happy. This was one of a number of factors which caused a dramatic fall in NUT membership in 1986 and 1987. It was ironic too that the NUT found itself attempting to impede the implementation of a reform of which it had been a leading advocate for fifteen years or more.

Further strike and non-strike action continued throughout the summer. An attempt by the smaller unions, led by the NASUWT, to link the 1985 pay settlement to the structure talks was vetoed by the NUT. It concentrated instead on trying to win individual local authorities to its claim. By the end of May over half of all local authorities – a number of them with new Labour majorities after the May elections – had endorsed the teachers' claim on the understanding that they thus became exempt from strike action. Sir Keith Joseph, however, continued to insist on the 4.0 per cent limit to any pay offer.

When the employers moved a little and offered 6.0 per cent with reform of the pay structure, it was no longer sufficient to satisfy any of the teachers' side. When Sir Keith offered a £1.25-billion settlement over four years linked to restructuring and new conditions, he too received short shrift. The NUT was locked into a demand that the 1985 pay claim should be settled before the wider issues were reopened. It also opposed – with the 1984 experience still fresh in mind – the NASUWT's proposal for arbitration.

Similarly, divisions were becoming increasingly apparent on the employers' side. The 1985 local elections had resulted in Labour taking control of the management panel. However, the 1965 Concordat was still in operation, under which the two DES representatives on Burnham were given a veto over the global sum. When that summer the DES and Conservative representatives voted together to block a new proposal put forward by the Labour side, informal talks between the latter and the unions began. Even when the management panel went as far as repudiating the Concordat with the DES, agreement remained remote. As a result, for the first time in history, a new school year began in September 1985 under the shadow of a dispute involving strike action.

The NUT began its ban on co-operation with the implementation of GCSE and a series of half-day and three-day strikes around the country. A forcefully worded motion supporting the teachers' case was debated and unanimously carried at the TUC in early September. When a new, improved offer of 6.9 per cent was made later in the month, the NASUWT and the smaller unions indicated they were prepared to accept it. The NUT was adamantly opposed to it and used its teachers' panel majority to rule it out of court. In a further ballot of NUT members there was a 76 per cent majority for half-day strikes, and in the week of 19–26 September there was a series of rallies around the country.

The strikes continued in October, but were beginning to take their toll. On 15 October the employers offered 6.9 per cent, endloaded to give 7.5 per cent by the end of the year. The offer also included a commitment to a Royal Commission on teachers' pay and a demand for an end to all action. While the other unions were prepared to accept this, they were outvoted in the teachers' panel by the NUT. Its reasons for opposing the settlement were clear; the deal would have done nothing about the erosion of teachers' pay or about the restoration of the Houghton levels. Furthermore, it would also have opened up non-Burnham negotiations and the linkage between pay and conditions which the employers wanted. Nevertheless, it was about as much as the employers could offer in their straitened circumstances, unless the government had provided more money, and the rejection resulted in many more months of deadlock.

Keith Joseph attempted to turn the decision against the teachers. They 'have chosen', he argued in the Commons, 'to continue to disrupt the education of the pupils in their charge rather than accept – or even discuss – the offer made to them. I deplore this, the damage it causes, and the example it sets' (Seifert, 1987, p. 214).

More damaging to the NUT than his words was his decision to alter the representation of the various unions on the teachers' panel. As a result the Union lost the majority it had held on Burnham since its creation. In November the NUT was outvoted for the first time, when the other five organizations combined to vote through on a 15 to 13 majority a decision to seek an interim settlement. There was no immediate response from the other side – the government showed no signs of providing extra resources – and sanctions, including bouts of strike action by the NUT and NASUWT, continued. Nevertheless, that vote marked the beginning of a period of isolation for the NUT.

However, the Union maintained the overwhelming support of its members. When the other five began discussions with the employers under the auspices of the Advisory Conciliation and Arbitration Service (ACAS), the NUT's special salaries conference on 18 January 1986 overwhelmingly supported the Executive's decision to keep out of the talks. Even after a deal had been struck, NUT members voted 3 to 1 in a ballot to continue in dispute.

The deal resulting from the talks was ratified by the Burnham Committee on 3 March 1986, the NUT being once again outvoted. It provided for 6.9 per cent backdated to April 1985 with an additional 1.6 per cent from March 1986. It also included the establishment, under the guidance of an ACAS panel, of talks on pay, conditions of service and future negotiating machinery. In short, it opened up the whole agenda.

The tensions within the teachers' side were transformed into a bitter public row. The NUT called the deal 'quite simply a sellout' (*NUT News* [1986] 4, p. 1). Fred Smithies, the General Secretary of the NASUWT, responded: 'I deeply regret that the NUT sought, by innuendo and lies, to distort our position' (Seifert, 1987, p. 226). The settlement was described by the NASUWT as a 'victory', and was supported by 69 per cent of its membership in a ballot (quoted in Seifert, 1987, p. 224). While such bitterness was understandable after the intensity of the conflict and though the leadership of each union probably judged correctly what they could 'sell' to their membership, the depth of the divisions on the teachers' side played into Kenneth Baker's hands. It was an important factor in allowing him to impose his own settlement and take away negotiating rights for teachers the following winter.

As the talks at ACAS developed it became clear to the NUT that it needed to find a way back in. Though it maintained its non-strike sanctions into the summer term, the public case was becoming harder to argue and their impact was waning. When, on 9 May 1986, an interim settlement of £520 or 5.5 per cent, whichever was the greater, was agreed, the NUT was able to accept it. It went some way towards the £800 interim award demanded by NUT Conference and allowed the NUT back into the ACAS talks. Sanctions were called off.

While the formula enabled progress on the broad agenda agreed earlier in the year to be made, it was by no means greeted with delight across the country. The nature of some of the sanctions created part of the problem. With GCSE being implemented on the government's timetable, two groups of members were angered: those who wanted to continue the campaign to delay its introduction; and those who had reluctantly but loyally stayed away from training and now faced teaching the new examination unprepared. There was also a substantial minority who believed that not enough had been gained to justify ending the dispute.

This group, led by the Socialist Teachers' Alliance (STA), remained fierce critics of the Union leadership, when in July 1986 they signed the Heads of Agreement at Coventry. This provided for a new salary structure based on an entry grade and a main professional grade (MPG) with two levels of allowance, which would be available to 15 per cent of the profession. It gave an average but unevenly distributed rise of 14 per cent in 1986–7. Importantly for its advocates, the agreement also provided for guaranteed non-contact time and the phased introduction of limits on class sizes. The STA were not the only critics of the proposed deal. The NASUWT opposed it because it took the view that the upper limit of £14,500 on the MPG was too low, while the DES believed it made inadequate provision for promoted posts within a cost package that was in any case too great. The relatively small proportion of posts of responsibility allowed for in the agreement was widely criticized.

In the first half of the autumn term the NUT leadership set out to sell the package to the profession. By contrast, the NASUWT had reverted to a series of half-day strikes in opposition to the deal. In November substantial advances were made on the Coventry deal when a more detailed agreement was reached in Nottingham. It provided for a higher maximum on the MPG, a 23½-hour upper limit on weekly contact time, and a National Joint Council for the future negotiation of teachers' pay and conditions.

The advances were not enough to satisfy the NASUWT, and the headteacher organizations were unhappy with them too. The NUT and AMMA, however, supported the agreement, though in the case of the NUT the support was hardly overwhelming. At its special salaries conference approval was given with a vote of 122,557 to 100,973. The ballot that followed revealed that the split ran right through the membership, as 42 per cent voted against the deal. Half-hearted or not, it was a 'yes' vote and in January, on the basis of the votes of the NUT and AMMA, the deal was ratified in both the Burnham Committee and CLEA/ST. By then, however, the agreement between the employers and the teachers had been overtaken by events.

The government had become increasingly anxious about its ability to influence negotiations from the moment the Concordat had been repudiated in July 1985. When the talks began at ACAS in 1986 they appeared, from the Secretary of State's angle, to be talks between Labour-controlled local authorities and radical teacher organizations, hardly a prospect likely to appeal to a government that had spent a good deal of energy attacking both.

From the autumn of 1986 onwards it was increasingly apparent that the government was planning the replacement of Burnham. As the autumn turned into winter, Kenneth Baker also made clear his opposition to the Coventry and then the Nottingham agreement. In November he threatened publicly that he intended to impose a deal which would provide for a much lower MPG, detailed contracts specifying teachers' duties, and the replacement of negotiating machinery with an Interim Advisory Committee appointed by him alone, which would make recommendations. His threat was a sword of Damocles over the Nottingham negotiations. The advocates of the Nottingham settlements argued that if they were not ratified it would allow Baker to impose his deal. The Queen's Speech, which included proposals to repeal the Remuneration of Teachers Act, confirmed the view. For the government, the divisions which had riven the unions for a year or more were a perfect pretext for arguing the case for repeal. Their continuation into early 1987 assisted the government in seeing their bill onto the statute book, the Nottingham agreement notwithstanding.

The Teachers' Pay and Conditions Act, which abolished teachers' negotiating rights and gave the Secretary of State for Education power to impose a settlement, became law on 2 March 1987. The same day, Kenneth Baker announced a settlement worth 16.4 per cent over two years, five levels of allowance and a detailed list of duties, including an obligation to work 1265 hours of directed time. This provoked an outburst of unity among the unions, and a wave of strikes organized by the NASUWT and the NUT, but they made no impact on the government. In any case, the unions were exhausted and the public confused.

Given the end result it is possible to see the period of industrial conflict as a disaster for the unions. In some senses it was: they were divided; some of their sanctions had caused confusion in the profession; their relations with the public were at best uncertain; their finances had been stretched; and their right to bargain collectively – a central trade union function – had gone. For the NUT there had been an alarming drop in membership, which caused it additional financial difficulties. The government, in the run-up to the general election in 1987, took full advantage of the teachers' weakness to announce the radical package of reforms which became the 1988 Education Reform Act.

On the other hand – particularly compared to some of the other disastrous trade union campaigns of the 1980s – the extent to which the teacher unions had succeeded should not be overlooked. The amount of money that Baker finally found for teachers' salaries was far in excess of the sums Sir Keith Joseph had proposed. This, at a time, as we have seen, of an ideological and economic commitment from the government to squeeze public expenditure, was a substantial gain. The unions had also successfully steered Sir Keith's 1984 talk of appraisal to weed out incompetent teachers into an agreement that provided for six pilot studies, which excluded the use of appraisal for punitive purposes or indeed as a mechanism for the award of pay.

It is also significant that teaching has emerged from the crisis of the 1980s as a highly unionized profession. Though the NUT saw its membership fall, partly because it carried burdens on behalf of the whole profession, the percentage of teachers in unions overall did not drop significantly. Finally, the industrial conflict had generated a level of public concern about the state of education which, though it has fluctuated, has remained high ever since. In the short term, the Conservative government was able to exploit this – and the weakness of the unions – to press through its market-style reform of the service. In the longer run, however, it has become clear that glossy plans and radical proposals of whatever political persuasion are no substitute for investment in the quality of the service. This became evident in 1990 as public concern at the government's handling of education grew steadily, to the extent that even the *Sun* published an editorial urging the government to invest more in teachers' pay. The main contribution, historically, of the mid-1980s may well be that it prompted politicians and the public to ask a series of questions about the future of publicly provided education. The answers to those questions remain highly controversial, but at least the issues are on the agenda of political and public debate.

The NUT's response to conflict

Having looked at the elements of the conflict, and the dispute that represented its peak, it is now necessary to attempt a brief analysis of the NUT's pattern of response to the period of conflict as a whole.

The first point to make is that there have been continuing ideological and tactical rifts within the NUT during the crisis. From the early 1970s, a 'Broad Left' alliance controlled the National Executive. As its name suggests, this grouping took in a wide range of views on the left of the political spectrum; it was broadly progressive and, to use Marxist terminology, reformist rather than revolutionary. Throughout the late 1970s and 1980s, the main challenge to this group came from the revolutionary left in the form of a variety of Trotskyite factions, the most successful of which was the STA. While these groups never came close to gaining a majority on the Executive, they exerted considerable influence in a number of branches, notably inner London. They were also capable of organizing sometimes successful challenges to the Executive's ruling group at Annual Conference.

The divisions between the two factions have sometimes damaged the Union's image, particularly when they were fought out in public or on occasions when the Union was in the public eye. Such divisions also at times hampered the policy development process in a way in which Kerchner and Mitchell identified in their research: 'agreements which satisfy all the factions within the union ... tend to be expensive and unwieldy. Bargaining theorists call this the problem of "side payments"' (Kerchner and Mitchell, 1988, p. 117). On the other hand, if proposals fail to satisfy all factions, then the controversy within the Union can undermine its attempts to campaign for the policy externally. Divisions of this nature also consume extensive amounts of the energy of hard-pressed elected members.

Again, though, it should be recognized that, in a time of rapidly changing circumstances – particularly when, as in the late 1970s and the 1980s, the changes are adverse for an organization – such conflicts are inevitable in democratic organizations and indeed to some extent a sign of continuing health. It should further be recognized that the issues at stake can be extremely important, and cannot always be attributed to 'political in-fighting' or personal rivalries. The nature of a pay claim, for example, or the best way of promoting it, are major issues. What kind of curriculum? In what way should teachers be held accountable? These too are crucial issues, to which a variety of responses is possible. Controversy and conflict may be seen as the price the NUT pays for its structures, which are highly democratic at all levels. For example, during the pay dispute of the mid-1980s, the NUT held no fewer than 14 ballots of its membership.

Nevertheless, it would be wrong to assume that as a result of internal debate the Union has had no direction through the period of conflict. On the contrary, it is possible to discern three distinct phases in its response to the onslaught it has faced since the late 1970s. Its initial response was straightforwardly defensive; the second phase might be described as pragmatic; while the third is described here as strategic. In suggesting this framework for analysing the Union's response to crisis, I am drawing heavily on Eric Hewton's analysis of the local authority response in *Education in Recession* (1986). Hewton describes the three phases as defensive, pragmatic and reformist. Rather than use all his titles, I have changed the last one because of its specific meaning in Marxist theory, a connotation which I do not think he intended, and which in any case I wish to avoid since it is inappropriate in this context. LEAs, as we have seen, faced an onslaught almost as severe as that faced by teachers' unions. It is not surprising, therefore, that the responses of the two partners to the crisis followed a similar pattern.

The defensive phase lasted well into the mid-1980s and assumed as its objective a return to the position which preceded the crisis. The Union's response to the winding up of the Schools' Council, and its refusal to open formal relations with its successor, the SCDC, exemplifies a defensive response. The second phase covered the latter part of the 1980s, including the passage of the Education Reform Act, during which the Union responded piecemeal to a series of government proposals without presenting a coherent alternative. Although during this period the irreversible nature of the crisis became apparent, the implicit assumption remained that the status quo prior to the crisis represented the ideal. Finally, the Union has recently begun to look beyond the immediate threat posed by government reforms and to map out an alternative direction. The assumption that the status quo ante was ideal has been rejected. Instead, the Union has begun to ask questions about the long-term future. What sort of education service is appropriate to the year 2000? What plan or strategy is suited to reaching that goal? This type of thinking is still embryonic within the Union, but there is a growing realization of its importance. The publication in 1990 of *A Strategy for the Curriculum* is indicative of this new phase (NUT, 1990a). What it might mean during the 1990s is explored fully in the section of Chapter 7 entitled 'The strategic union'.

6 Influence

The first five chapters of this book have examined the development of the NUT from its foundation in 1870 through to the present day. Its campaigns and their effects have been evaluated. The focus in this chapter is the means by which the NUT – and other unions – influence their employers, the government and the decision-making process in general. To some extent these have changed over time, though, as the chapter will demonstrate, there has been a remarkable consistency in the use and effectiveness of some of those means throughout the Union's history. What does become clear is that the choice of which means to use depends upon the circumstances of the time; the attitude of the government and employers, the state of public concern and the economic prosperity or otherwise of the country. In short, the NUT, like others, in addition to deciding what its aims are, must also make strategic and tactical decisions about how to pursue them. This chapter looks at the strategic and tactical options available, and at the factors which influence union leaders to select one as opposed to another.

Before the various options are examined, they are set in a theoretical framework. The reader interested purely in information about teacher unions might therefore skip the first section of the chapter. However, power and influence, and the way in which they are wielded, are conceptually complex subjects, and the theoretical discussion which follows is intended to offer a deeper insight into them than a purely practical approach could provide.

Decision-making and the dimensions of power

Very little of the literature on teacher unions in this country draws explicitly on the important academic debate about decision-making and power. Coates' study of the shifts of policy in the NUT and other teacher organizations during the 1960s looks at teacher unions as examples of interest groups. He shows how their 'changing emphasis in both strategies and tactics ... were the product of changes in government policy ... and of changes in the accessibility of the Department [of Education and Science]' (Coates, 1972, p. 125). He argues convincingly that the behaviour of teacher organizations is a product both of external environmental factors and of internal organizational factors. He concludes by predicting that as a result on the one hand of increasingly militant demands from union members, and on the other of constraints on likely expenditure on education, 'the scene appears set for successive confrontations ... in the 1970s' (Coates, 1972, p. 127). As the previous chapter shows, Coates' analysis proved to be remarkably accurate, though the culmination of the conflict occurred in the 1980s. His study was therefore an important development. However, while his analysis of the NUT as an interest group is important, he does not explore in depth the concept of power or the different levels at which it is exercised. He does not, for example, explore why certain educational questions enter the political arena and others do not, nor how the demands that are made in a democratic society are shaped by those who control or influence what information surfaces in the public domain.

Kogan, on the other hand, in his important study *Educational Policy-Making* (1975), begins to enter these areas of debate. His extremely thorough research involved examining what educational issues had arisen during the 1960s and early 1970s, and then assessing which of a range of organizations had promoted these issues. It therefore represented a major advance and assists in explaining many important aspects of the decision-making process. His work, which is based on a pluralist approach to the study of power, is examined further in the next sub-section. This is followed by an examination of the main weaknesses of the approach and an explanation of the concept of non-decision-making and what Stephen Lukes describes as the second dimension of power (Lukes, 1974). Then Lukes' analysis of power, which – successfully in my view – attempted to go beyond those of both the pluralists and their critics, is explained.

The one-dimensional view

Any analysis of power must answer three apparently straightforward questions. What is power? Who wields it? For what purpose or purposes? In practice, once these questions are approached in anything but the most superficial way, the answers prove complex, controversial, and indeed 'essentially contested' (Lukes, 1974, p. 9).

The most straightforward approach, and indeed arguably the one that has led to the most valuable empirical research, is the one adopted by the pluralists, an approach dubbed 'one-dimensional' by Lukes. The virtues of the approach are twofold. Firstly it adopts a simple definition of power: in Dahl's words, 'A has power over B to the extent that he can get B to do something that B would not otherwise do' (quoted in Lukes, 1974, p. 12). Secondly it focuses analysis on clear-cut examples of the exercise of power. Again in Dahl's words, the pluralists aim to 'determine for each decision which participants had initiated alternatives that were finally adopted, had vetoed alternatives initiated by others, or had proposed alternatives that were turned down' (*ibid.*). This is the approach Kogan and his team adopted in *Educational Policy-Making* (Kogan, 1975), in which they sought the contentious issues of the period under study and then examined the extent to which each of the actors in the conflict wielded power.

In a sense, therefore, the pluralist approach can be said to be based on scientific method at least to the extent to which it focuses on observable behaviour. The problem with the approach is that because it focuses on observable conflict, it inevitably leads to the implicit assumption that when there is no such conflict, there must be agreement. Furthermore, it ignores the extent to which it is possible – as history demonstrates – for one group or class to manipulate another or others so that any conflict is not apparent. In short, it assumes that if individuals or groups have interests, they will express them in policy preferences. This presents numerous problems in relation to any analysis of policy-making. It is perhaps particularly acute in relation to education; children, for example, clearly have interests, but how can they be expected to express them as policy preferences? Since they cannot do so, it is not surprising that other actors tend to claim they are acting on their behalf. Thus although the pluralist position has the advantage of using scientific method, it has to be rejected as an adequate tool on its own for the analysis of power. Just because it is difficult to study power relations which do not result in observable conflict is not a reason for not attempting to do so.

The two-dimensional approach

The pluralist or one-dimensional analysis of power made a major contribution to understanding its operation, and perhaps as a result revealed its own inadequacies. Dahl himself acknowledged that one measure of a person's influence might be the ability to initiate 'a policy where no opposition appears' (Dahl, 1961, p. 66), a clear acknowledgement that the study of power must extend beyond the study of overt conflict.

Into this crack in the pluralist position, Bachrach and Baratz (1962) drove a sizeable wedge. They accepted that the winner of an observable conflict had power, but argued that this was only one aspect of it. 'Power is also exercised', they argued, 'when A devotes his energies to creating or re-inforcing social and political values and institutional practices that limit the scope of the political process to public consideration of only those issues which are comparatively innocuous to A.' In short, 'to the extent that a person or group ... creates or reinforces barriers to public airing of policy conflicts, that person has power' (quoted

77

in Lukes, 1974, p. 16). On the basis of this analysis, they develop the concept of the non-decision, which is defined as 'a decision that results in suppression or thwarting of a manifest challenge to the values or interests of the decision-maker' (*ibid.*, p. 18).

They acknowledge, therefore, the ability of those in power to influence the political agenda by deciding not only what is on it, but also what issues are left off it. After a decade of educational reform in England and Wales, during which many educationalists have admitted that part of the government's success has been to set the agenda, leaving others simply to respond, the analysis of Bachrach and Baratz must be acknowledged to be an improvement on the pluralists' position. Nevertheless, it too has difficulties. They insist, for example, that non-decisions can be studied because they can be observed in the same way as decisions can. Their analysis requires the identification of potential issues which, as a result of the conscious or unconscious action of those in power, do not 'gain access to the relevant decision-making arena'. They argue, however, that at some level there must be 'conflict, overt or covert'. If there is none, 'the presumption must be that there is consensus ... in which case non-decision-making is impossible', but how can this be squared with their assertion that non-decision-making is 'a means by which demands for change in the existing allocation of benefits and privileges in the community can be suffocated before they are even voiced' (quoted in Lukes, 1974, pp. 18–19)?

This last statement is crucial. While it reveals the advance they have made from the pluralists' position (power can make possible the exclusion of some issues from the agenda), it also identifies the flaw in their argument. What if there is no conflict to observe because some groups are not only unable to force their grievances onto the agenda, but are actually unaware of what their grievances are, or even whether they have any? According to Bachrach and Baratz, this must be assumed to represent consensus. It was in order to rectify this weakness that Lukes proposed the three-dimensional view.

The three-dimensional view

It is widely accepted that those in power hold on to it not only by winning when there is conflict, not only by successfully manipulating the political agenda, but also through 'the bias of the system', which is sustained 'most importantly, by the socially structured and culturally patterned behaviour of groups, and practices of institutions which may indeed be manifested by individuals' inaction'. As Lukes goes on to explain, 'A may exercise power over B by getting him to do what he does not want to do, but he also exercises power over him by influencing, shaping or determining his very wants' (Lukes, 1974, p. 22). While this may cause methodological problems for those who study power, since it requires an attempt to identify the 'real' as opposed to 'expressed' interests of individuals or groups, few surely would dispute the argument. Nor should the methodological difficulty deter people from either believing it to be the case, or indeed attempting to study power of this sort. The third dimension of power is particularly important in a study of power in education, for the education system has historically been a central means of 'influencing, shaping or determining [a person's] very wants'. Even Dahl, the leading pluralist, acknowledges this when he points out that 'almost the entire adult population has been subjected to some degree of indoctrination through the schools' (Dahl, 1961, p. 317).

This is not an issue simply in totalitarian states. The power of education to shape people's wants has been acknowledged throughout the history of education in the UK and has been a factor in many important decisions. The decision to establish national pay scales, for example, after the First World War was motivated, at least in part, by the Conservative government's fear that schools, through the teacher unions, would come under the control of the labour movement.

The third dimension of power is also vital to the effective study of trade unions in general, since they often find themselves countering employers and/or governments that are well placed to mobilize the bias of the system. Since in a conflict the battle to mobilize public opinion can be crucial, a study of unions which ignored the third dimension would be inadequate. This would be particularly acute in the case of teacher unions, which do not have the economic clout of those industrial unions whose strikes can cost employers millions of pounds each day in lost production.

For both these reasons, and because the case Lukes makes has not been effectively challenged, the three-dimensional framework for the analysis of power is adopted for the rest of this chapter.

Power: Dimension One

As we have seen, Lukes describes the pluralists' view of power as the first dimension. It should be noticed that he does not reject their notion of power per se, rather he sees it as being insufficient on its own. It is the purpose in this section to look at the NUT in this dimension, in which it is seen as overtly exercising power as an interest group. Analysis of the effectiveness of trade unions in general or teacher unions in particular rarely seems to delve beyond this first dimension. For this reason, the examination of union methods and activity in this dimension is necessarily lengthy.

One additional point of criticism of the pluralists needs to be added. There is a tendency for trade unions to be lumped together with other interest groups as if they are organizations of the same order. This is not the case. Firstly, they tend to have greater breadth than many interest groups, with an interest in many aspects of policy rather than focusing on one. Compare, for example, the range of concerns of the teacher unions with a subject association such as the Historical Association or the Association of Science Education. In 1990 the Historical Association welcomed the final report of the DES Working Group on the History National Curriculum because it took the view that it had resolved the various philosophical debates about history in schools. On the other hand, all the teacher organizations opposed it not only on historical grounds, but also because they saw the extent of its prescription as reducing the discretion and hence the motivation of their members. Furthermore, they were concerned about the workload it implied when set in the context of the rest of the proposed National Curriculum.

The second distinction between unions and interest groups is both philosophical and legal. Teacher unions represent their members in the workplace. Other interest groups rarely have this role. The involvement in the employer–employee relationship affects the nature of a union as an organization in human rights terms. More importantly, it also means they are subject to a range of both case and statute laws affecting the way they operate. The Employment Acts of the 1980s with their requirements for strike ballots, election of General Secretaries and restrictions on secondary action, for example, are particularly significant.

With these distinctions in mind, it is possible to examine the methods that teacher unions use in order to exercise power, or to resist the exercise of power by government and employers. Perhaps the most obvious method for trade unions is the strike, or withdrawal of labour. It should be recognized that historically speaking this is relatively rare in the case of teachers and normally only a tool of last resort. After the severe conflicts of the mid-1980s this is too easily forgotten. The first national strike in the history of the NUT was in 1969, though there have been several examples of national action since then. Local strikes are more common, but still, relative to many other industries, rare. There were, for example, NUT strikes in Brent and Haringey in 1988.

One reason for the rarity is the double-edged nature of the weapon. As in the case of all strikes, once labour is withdrawn, salary is forfeited. Thus either the employee, or the union which provides sustentation to strikers, or sometimes both, come under financial pressure. In industrial settings there is a reciprocal pressure on the employer, who loses production, and the victory in the conflict depends to a considerable extent on who is able to survive the pressure best. In the case of teachers' strikes, however, the employer does not suffer a loss of production in this sense. Pupils are sent home but there is no calculable financial cost to the employers. On the contrary, the employer, relieved of paying the teachers' salaries, actually improves its financial circumstances the longer the strike goes on. The balance of forces in a teachers' strike is therefore quite different from that in a conventional industrial setting.

Another major risk with engaging in strike action is the inconvenience it causes for teachers' potential allies – parents. It was clear, for example, during the long-running pay dispute of the mid-1980s, that many parents became exasperated with the constant action which inevitably interrupted their own work patterns. That is not to say that parents will always oppose strike action; indeed, as we have seen – at Lowestoft classically (see Chapter 2), but also in many other places – they can be decisive in bringing victory for teachers. It is to say that unless there is careful preparation, relationships can become strained. Furthermore, because teachers' strikes clearly impinge on children and damage their education, striking teachers are open to accusations of picking on 'innocent victims' and of not taking their professional responsibilities – they are after all *in loco parentis* – seriously enough. Responding to such accusations often requires conveying a message regarding, say, the long-term quality of provision which is more complex to explain than the obvious short-term damage caused by the strike.

Since the strike cannot succeed by damaging the economic prospects of the employer, the battle for the hearts and minds of parents and the community is the decisive factor. If the public can be persuaded that the government or the employers are responsible, then teachers have a chance of victory. If not, their chances are slim.

This is particularly so because it is not always easy to achieve united teacher support for strike action. This is partly because there are six different organizations representing teachers, but also because many teachers are reluctant to strike because of the nature of their work. As we have seen, teacher strikes are historically very rare, and normally result from either extreme provocation (as in Durham; see Chapter 4), or the breach of a basic trade union right (unfair dismissal, for example), or a complete breakdown of relations associated with a deep-rooted conflict (as in the mid-1980s). Maintaining unity behind a strike can be particularly difficult in a rural area with many small schools, in each of which the teachers are isolated from their colleagues and closely related to the village community. For all these reasons the strike weapon is a double-edged sword, though one which, if used carefully, can be highly effective. In recent years successful local strikes, such as those in Brent in 1988 or Hackney in 1990, had a sharp focus, united backing and brief duration. In Hackney, for example, only some 120 teachers who had been incorrectly paid by the new education authority were called out. Conversely, there is no evidence that unfocused strikes, perhaps of a demonstrative or protest nature, without united support, have any significant effect. The NASUWT's one-day protest in the spring of 1990 is a case in point.

Within the NUT, ballots before taking action began long before they became legally required. Nevertheless, the ballot is now a major tactical consideration. Unions are reluctant to call a ballot unless they are confident of overwhelming support for action. A slender majority, or even worse a defeat, on an action ballot severely weakens a union's negotiating position. On the other hand, a large majority in favour of action can be a strong card for negotiators to play, perhaps making a settlement possible without the action having to take place. In the NUT, decisions authorizing action must be taken at national level: local branches have no such power. This enables the Union to examine the broader strategic and national implications of strike action on any given question.

There are other forms of 'industrial' action which have been used by teachers to exert influence. It should be remembered, however, that any action involving breach of contract now requires, like strike action, a ballot, and therefore the same tactical considerations must be taken into account. Before the government-imposed contract of 1987, the withdrawal of good will or refusal to do the paradoxically named 'voluntary duties' was a key tactic in the dispute. Teachers refused to supervise lunch hours or attend parents' evenings, for example. School meals had been a long-running source of conflict, and were at the heart of a major dispute in the 1960s. Though the imposition of a contract in the 1980s brought to an end the use of an often effective tactic – which crucially did not involve loss of salary – it also resulted in a permanent loss of good will on the part of teachers, whose resentment of it remains to this day. As a tactic it had the disadvantage that while it caused irritation or inconvenience, the threat it posed was limited. It lent itself, therefore, more to the guerilla campaign than the decisive victory, yet long conflicts, as we have seen, tend to work against teachers' interests.

Teachers' unions have a range of other tactics in the armoury. One which has been used to some effect throughout the history of the NUT is a boycott on applications for posts in an authority. Advertisements sponsored by three major unions recommending members not to apply for jobs in Brent appeared early in 1990. The NUT threatened similar action against Hackney in July 1990. This type of action has historically proved highly successful. Naturally, its influence is all the greater when unions work together to enforce it.

Often action of these kinds will be associated with direct campaigning work. This may involve demonstrations, petitions, leafleting, lobbies and so on. We have seen in previous chapters how historically the NUT used lobbying techniques at national level. It should not be forgotten that such lobbying is a routine part of local relations between the Union and local authorities. In 1989, for example, the NUT Division in Hackney organized a highly successful lobby of the new authority, in which it persuaded enough Labour councillors to defy the whip and agree to substantial teacher representation on the new Education Committee. At local level effective lobbying has a real chance of success, especially where a council is hung or, paradoxically, where one party has a massive majority and is therefore prone to splits from time to time.

National-level campaigning has perhaps been less successful in the last decade or so, though not without its effect. The NUT campaigned intensively against the Education Reform Act, but even with the broad alliances it built with the local authorities and others, it affected the final Act less than Baroness Cox did, working alone. The campaigns during the pay dispute of the 1980s certainly contributed to its achievements, particularly the reaching of an agreement with the local authorities. Campaigning activity can also have beneficial effects in building solidarity and commitment among teachers. Many teachers remember with affection the closeness with colleagues that was achieved at times during the conflict of the 1980s. Again, such solidarity is clearly much easier to achieve where unions co-operate at school level, or where one union has an overwhelming preponderance of members. Campaigns on issues which are not highly contentious politically have also succeeded. The NUT had considerable success in 1989–90 in campaigning for more effective support for women who wanted to return to the profession. Similarly, in 1991 its campaign for teachers with disabilities brought about important changes in government policy.

The processes of campaigning and lobbying have become much more complex and sophisticated. Patterns which have been common in the United States for a generation or more have mushroomed in the United Kingdom in the last decade. Consultant MPs, who are paid a fee in return for ensuring that the Union's concerns are raised on the appropriate Parliamentary occasions, go back many years, and are widely used.

Increasingly, however, professional PR campaigns have been employed to extend Union campaigns. In the autumn of 1989, and again in 1990, the NUT ran a series of full-page newspaper advertisements as part of its campaign for improved teachers' pay. In September 1990 it ran a billboard advertising campaign on a similar theme. In 1988 the Union was relaunched with a new logo in an attempt to present a new image. In each case PR companies were engaged to use their sophisticated skills of assessing public opinion and designing advertising images accordingly. In Massachusetts, the Teachers' Association has already turned to hard-hitting television advertising. I would predict that it will only be a matter of time before British teacher unions follow suit, but the cost of it may require them to collaborate on such a project. This theme will be picked up again later in this chapter; once campaigning moves into this area, it is no longer a traditional pluralist response to government action, but an attempt at a much more subtle level to shape public opinion in the second and third dimensions of power.

Before turning to those, one other important aspect of teacher union influence of a traditional pluralist nature requires examination. Kogan (1975) draws a distinction between legitimized and non-legitimized interest groups. The former, he argues, have established a right to be consulted in the policy formation process. The NUT, on this basis, has been legitimized since the appointment of George Kekewich to the Board of Education in 1890. Even during the assault on teacher union influence during the 1980s, that legitimacy has been maintained. The NUT continues to make detailed responses to government circulars and to proposals from, for example, the NCC or the SEAC. Its responses are no doubt considered; some bring about alteration in proposals, and a few, even in the current hostile climate, result in retractions and withdrawals of proposals. Some of the NUT's proposals on the National Curriculum in mathematics, for example, appear in the final orders. The retraction of proposals for the Annual Curriculum Return in early 1990 also clearly resulted from teacher union pressure. As we have seen, the NUT publication *Opening Doors* (NUT, 1989b), on encouraging returners to the profession, was acknowledged by the government and resulted in £10 million being provided for such programmes in the government's 1990 Education Grants Programme.

From time to time the Union presents its response orally in a deputation to the DES or to the Secretary of State. These too can be influential. The NUT's deputation during the consultations on teacher appraisal in 1989–90 undoubtedly heightened government awareness of the pitfalls of some of the proposals it was considering. Further deputations demonstrably influenced Kenneth Clarke's (the Secretary of State for Education from November 1990) proposals on teacher appraisal in December 1990 and July 1991. Through this kind of work, the NUT plays, on behalf of teachers, an advocate role of which even many of its members may be unaware. Yet, in many ways, its role in protecting and promoting the interests of members is more important than much of the higher-profile work. To carry out this role effectively, a teacher union requires access to high levels of expertise among staff and members, and a degree of policy consistency without which its views are unlikely to be taken seriously.

Power: Dimension Two

Attempts to influence policy in the traditional pluralist way, by exerting pressure on government, inevitably overlap with attempts by teacher unions to force particular issues onto the political or policy-making agenda. Bachrach and Baratz argue that power is also exercised when 'a person or group . . creates or reinforces barriers to the public airing of policy conflicts' (quoted in Lukes, 1974, p. 16). This 'non-decision-making' is described by Lukes as the second dimension of power. It has significance for teacher unions in two ways; firstly, they attempt to force items onto the agenda that the government does not want aired; secondly, they in turn attempt to exert influence to keep certain uncomfortable items off the public agenda.

Teacher unions have a number of means at their disposal if they seek to establish on the public and political agenda an item they consider the government would prefer to exclude from it. One option is to demand an inquiry or a more permanent consultative body. For example, ever since 1987, when the government reformed the funding of in-service education (INSET), the unions have demanded the establishment of a consultative forum on in-service education for teachers, in which they hope to open up a debate about national priorities for INSET expenditure. The government, however, keen to maintain control over priorities, has so far refused to countenance such a body. In the past when such bodies have been established, unions have been able to exert a powerful influence, as the Schools' Council, for example, demonstrates.

A second option available to unions is to exploit openings made for them by others. One item of major concern to unions over the 1980s has been the deteriorating quality of school buildings. The government for its part, intent on restricting public expenditure, would prefer to keep so expensive an item off the agenda. The best opportunities the NUT has had to raise the profile of this issue have been presented by the annual reports from HMI on the quality of provision. The 1985 HMI Report (DES, 1986) was, for example, followed up by the NUT with a leaflet which quoted extensively from it. Other opportunities on this question have been offered by DES estimates of the necessary expenditure to repair the current stock of buildings, while at local level, an LEA's annual capital programme proposals provide an opportunity to raise the issue. The National Audit Office report on school buildings in the summer of 1991 provided a further opportunity to press the government on the issue.

Nevertheless, the government has probably been more successful than the unions on this question. One way it has done this is simply by pressing forward with a series of proposals which dominate the agenda to the extent that time and energy for other matters is in short supply.

The question of school buildings is but one example of many which could be cited. Another was the attempt to generate concern about teachers' pay and conditions after Sir Claus Moser's speech to the British Association conference in late August 1990 (Moser, 1990). Moser's speech, which called for the establishment of a Royal Commission on Education, generated interest in educational issues well beyond the education service, and may force issues onto the political agenda regardless of government, or for that matter union, efforts. It will be interesting to see whether the privately funded Education Commission, which has resulted from the Moser speech, is indeed able to shift the agenda.

A third way to promote an issue on to the agenda is to issue a major policy statement on it. During the height of the controversy on the government's education reforms, for example, the NUT produced publications on subjects such as *Meeting Special Needs in Ordinary Schools* (NUT, 1989a), *Towards Equality for Girls and Boys* (NUT, 1988) and *Begin at the Beginning* (NUT, 1989c). All of these were attempts to take the initiative and promote, with varying degrees of success, issues of concern to members that were in danger of being neglected. In 1990, the NUT launched its major curriculum policy document, *A Strategy for the Curriculum* (1990a), and began a widespread campaign on it. Here there was no need to ensure the item was on the agenda; instead the aim was to change the terms of reference of the debate, so that it was structured less around government proposals and more around what kind of education service was required in the 1990s.

The success of such campaigns depends to some extent on the level of media interest in them. The unions normally find that the government is able to exert much greater influence on the media than they are. This is not only because a government proposal is intrinsically more likely to generate interest than a union proposal, but also because very often the union message is likely to be predictable and therefore less 'newsworthy'. Importantly too, in times of Conservative government at any rate, the political links between government and much of the press operate against the unions. On the other hand, a campaign can have long-term influence on the education service in spite of a lack of interest from the media. If, for example, substantial numbers of educational academics become involved with an issue, this helps to set parameters for educational debate in the longer term.

These same pressures make it hard for unions to keep off the agenda items which the government want aired. Nevertheless, there are examples of the unions attempting to do so success-fully. We have seen, for example, the extent to which the cur-riculum was simply not a matter for discussion for almost twenty years after the Second World War. More recently, the unions have attempted to marginalize proposals for regional pay as a solution to teacher shortage.

The extent of the NUT's influence over the policy agenda has been greatly reduced as a result of the change of governmental attitude outlined in Chapter 5. Divisions between the teacher unions and within them can also result in issues reaching the agenda when one union or the majority of a union's Executive would prefer that they did not. For all these reasons, in the second dimension of power – control of the agenda – the government has been the dominant influence in recent years. In order to challenge this dominance the NUT has begun to explore other ways of influencing the agenda. One way has been to attempt to generate public concern through advertising and other techniques. There is no doubt, for example, that the Union's 1989 newspaper advertisements helped to raise public awareness of teacher shortage. The other method which the NUT has embarked upon in its campaign on the curriculum is to attempt to think strategically and thus to leap out of the strait-jacket of the short term. It is precisely in these respects that the NUT is seeking ways of competing with the government in what Lukes has described as the third dimension of power.

Power: Dimension Three

As we have seen, the authorities and teacher unions conflict both overtly over issues, and less overtly over the control of the decision-making agenda. Increasingly, however, there is conflict at a third and deeper level. That governments in the twentieth century have become more and more sophisticated in determin-ing people's perceptions of their own needs and interests is well known. Such attempts, while often associated with totalitarian regimes, are by no means confined to them. There are many examples in flourishing democracies, including the United Kingdom in the 1980s, of attempts to influence the media, to suppress uncomfortable reports and to manipulate the information on the basis of which people formulate their demands on the political system. All political parties now take great care to examine their presentation of policy in attempts to influence people – voters – at both conscious and subconscious levels.

Until recently, however, this has been terrain on which teacher unions have not chosen to fight. Its increasingly obvious importance, the growing skill of government in using it and the relative failure of teacher unions at other levels of power have, however, led the NUT to begin to compete at this level. The growing interest in advertising and sophisticated PR techniques can only be explained in this context. The sketch in Chapter 7 of a strategic union builds on the assumption that competing with the government in the third dimension of power will be an essential component of success in the 1990s.

There are two aspects of the growing conflict at this level. On the one hand there is competition for the hearts and minds of 'the public' over what their educational demands should be. As an example, is 'choice' really what parents want, or would they prefer simply to be confident that their local school was an excellent school?

Secondly, and more insidiously, there is increasing evidence of government interest in influencing the demands of voters in the future by manipulating the content and nature of the curriculum now. As Dahl (1961, p. 317) has pointed out, schooling is a powerful influence on people's thinking: 'almost the entire adult population has been subjected to some degree of indoctrination through the schools'. Should any government prove successful in influencing the curriculum for political rather than educational reasons, it would pose a threat to democracy itself.

How a teacher union might begin to challenge the government effectively – with its extensive influence over the media – in the third dimension of power is a major strategic question which is explored in the next chapter.

7 Strategic teacher unionism?

There is an extensive literature on the development of teacher unions in England and Wales. In this concluding chapter, the first purpose is to examine the extent to which writers on teacher unionism in the UK have explained the process of teacher union development as opposed to simply telling the story. The second purpose is to explore in some depth the recently initiated, but extremely important, international debate about a new or professional model of teacher unionism. Thirdly, the implications of recent changes in legislation for teacher unions are surveyed. Finally, drawing on all of this and the analysis in Chapters 5 and 6, there is a speculative attempt to analyse the prospects for teacher unions in England and Wales into the next century and to define strategic teacher unionism.

Accounts of teacher unionism in England and Wales

In attempting to examine the way in which previous writers have explored the process of teacher union development in England and Wales, it should be admitted at the outset that some of them made no attempt to establish any model. It will be argued, however, that in these cases there are assumptions, to some extent implicit, which underpin their historical accounts.

Before turning to the accounts themselves, it is also worth justifying the attempt to find some kind of model or pattern of development. We live, after all, in a culture with a strong attachment to pragmatic history and a generally suspicious view of theory. The first reason for the attempt is that there clearly are patterns, or at least similarities, in the development of western education systems. The relationship of teachers and their organizations to the common elements ought, therefore, to be identifiable. Secondly, and this is important for teachers in the 1990s, there are important strategic decisions to be made currently about the future of the teaching profession. How should teachers and their unions select from among the many possible futures? There will be a debate about what sort of future teachers want. There will also be a debate about the strategies required to move them towards it. Neither of these sets of decisions will be straightforward; the education system in England and Wales (and it is not alone) is at a turning point. There is a great deal of uncertainty about the choices teachers collectively should make. It is therefore surely a worthwhile and urgent task to try to sift the history of a teacher union and the interpretations of that history for assistance in making those choices.

The two most important accounts of the history of the teaching profession in England and Wales are provided by Asher Tropp in *The School Teachers* (1957) and Peter Gosden in *The Evolution of a Profession* (1972). Both are indispensable, highly readable, detailed accounts of the history, and both make implicit assumptions about the direction of history. Tropp's book, published in 1957, argues on page 3 that the profession 'slowly and as the result of prolonged effort has won free and reached a position of self-government and independence'. It concludes with a section entitled 'Towards Professional Status', and argues that 'the movement towards professional status and professional self-government still continues' (p. 267). This is the key to his approach. His outstanding narrative account assumes a linear process of development from poor and oppressed status in the nineteenth century to the brink of full professional status in the 1950s. In short, the model he implicitly proposes is of the 'onward and upward' variety, a classic Whig approach to history.

There are serious problems with this view. As Martin Lawn has pointed out,

> Tropp was in effect arguing that various strikes, pay campaigns, economic and political alliances and a cross-party non-political interest group approach over a timespan of a hundred years was all part of a conscious effort to achieve occupational freedom ... This is a difficult argument to develop, it is ahistorical and positivist, held together by the social and political circumstances of its time. (Lawn, 1990)

Lawn's concluding sentence provides the key to another problem. While at the time Tropp wrote – with the teaching profession in full post-1944-Act bloom – the assumptions of steady improvement made common sense, the thirty or so years since then have given the lie to them. In particular, the challenge of the 1980s to the teacher unions, which evidently threatened their strength and forced them into retreat, makes Tropp's view untenable.

Very much the same criticism can be made of Gosden's work. Though his book, *The Evolution of a Profession*, was published fifteen years later than Tropp's, as we have seen, it coincided with a period of relative success for the teacher unions. Indeed, as Gosden points out, it coincided with the point in history at which the Secretary of State for Education required a specific course of training for graduates entering the profession. 'At last the aim of those teachers' associations which have sought to close the profession to any who have not taken a specific course of training in teaching has been achieved' (Gosden, 1972, p. 310). Furthermore, while Gosden's is a meticulous piece of historical work, it too has a tendency to assume that the teaching profession, largely through the efforts of the teacher organizations, was involved in a steady rise in status.

Walter Roy's book, *The Teachers' Union* (1968) provides a vital insider's view of the NUT in the 1950s and 1960s. As a leading activist and member of the Union's Executive, he was in position to provide many insights that neither Tropp nor Gosden could have given. It is a fascinating descriptive study. How-

ever, it is clear too that Roy makes implicit assumptions similar
to those of Tropp and Gosden. He clearly argues that the NUT
should develop as a professional organization rather than on the
model of an industrial union. Hence he argues forcefully against
the NUT joining the TUC. He also assumes that the Union's
history had led inexorably to the peak it had reached at the time
he was writing.

Furthermore, he offers little analysis of the ways in which the
NUT was able to influence policy, or of the extent to which the
Union, as opposed to other factors, brought about its achievements. The choice of the Durham dispute in the 1950s, in which
the NUT opposed the enforcement of the closed shop, is characteristic of his approach. It was a dispute in which the NUT allied
itself to established professions such as doctors and called on
government to assist it in a conflict with a local authority. Furthermore, it demonstrated the Union's political independence,
since it involved conflict with a Labour local authority (see
Chapter 4). Yet in many ways the Durham dispute is an excep-
tion in the history of the NUT; as we have seen, most disputes in
its history have involved conflict with local authorities aiming to
keep public expenditure down, either to keep rates low or
because of restrictions on central government's contribution to
local expenditure. In short, while Roy's work is a fascinating
snapshot from one of the leading protagonists in the NUT's
debates of the time, it does not assist in unravelling the process,
over the longer term, of teacher union development.

Coates, whose work was examined earlier (in Chapter 6),
provides a valuable insight into shifts in teacher union policy in
the 1960s and the reasons for them. In demonstrating the effects
of changes in government attitude and indeed of broader economic developments, Coates indicates a more subtle model of
teacher union development than do Tropp and Gosden. Here
there is no assumption that the teacher unions will necessarily
continue to progress in the direction of full professional status.
The importance of the relationship between the teacher organizations and the state is demonstrated, and an explanation for the

nature of the relationship provided. The different responses of the various teacher associations are explained in terms of internal organizational factors.

However, Coates was more concerned with teacher organizations as examples of interest groups in action. His aim was to draw conclusions about the influence of environmental and organizational factors in governing interest group behaviour. His book does not, therefore, attempt to explain the longer-term process of development of the NUT or the other teacher organizations.

Lawn and Ozga in *Teachers, Professionalism and Class* (1981), by contrast, are intent on drawing generalizable lessons from a study of a specific period of history. Their particular concern is to explain that the term 'professional' is contested and therefore used differently by teachers and the state and at different historical junctures. They argue that the government's offering to teachers of at least an element of 'professional status' in the aftermath of the First World War was an explicit element in a strategy designed to detach teachers from a dangerous liaison with the working class and the socialist movement.

Their analysis of the term 'professionalism' is a major step forward in understanding the history of teacher unions. It undermines significantly the work of Tropp and Gosden, who use the term indiscriminately. However, their broader analysis is flawed. Throughout, it is apparent that they believe organized teachers would have been better off had they thrown in their lot with the labour movement rather than heeding government promises of professional status. The case for this view is unproven at best. Certainly, as Tropp demonstrates, teachers on the whole fared better through the inter-war depression than many other groups. Would they have fared better had they been more closely aligned to the labour movement, which was decimated in the years following 1926? Lawn and Ozga would need to face up to uncomfortable questions such as this.

The second major weakness of Lawn and Ozga's work is that they appear throughout to take a monolithic view of the state.

They make no distinction between different types of state. Is there no distinction to be made between, say, a democratically elected government and a dictatorship? For public sector employees such as teachers, attitudes to different types of state are not simply a matter of academic interest. Furthermore, Lawn and Ozga appear to make no distinction between the state at local and at national level. Yet many of the conflicts in which teachers have been involved have been associated with conflicts between local and central government. At different times, teacher unions have allied themselves with central government against local government (the Durham dispute, for example) or with local government against the centre (during the pay dispute in 1985–6, for example). If no distinction is made, as in Lawn and Ozga's work, then much of teacher union history becomes incomprehensible.

Lawn himself recognizes this in his later book, *Servants of the State* (1987), in which he refines the views of the earlier volume. The work on the contested meaning of professionalism is advanced. On the basis of the evidence, Lawn is able to show that the attitude of central government in the 1920s was to manage teachers on the model of 'indirect rule', which Lugard and others had applied so successfully in colonial policy. In this process the concept of professionalism – as defined by government – was critical. *Servants of the State* is probably the most effective study to date of any period of teacher union history in England and Wales. More such studies are required if we are to make sense of teacher history in the UK. The crisis of the 1980s requires a radical re-examination of the one hundred and twenty years of teacher union history, since the confidence exemplified by Tropp and Gosden can no longer be assumed. In any case, there is currently in progress an incipient international debate about the development of teacher unions, which focuses not only on the past but also on its lessons for the future. This debate is the theme of the next section.

Generational development and professional unionism

The most important contribution to the present controversy about the process of teacher union development is *The Changing Idea of a Teachers' Union* by Charles Kerchner and Douglas Mitchell (1988). Indeed, this seminal book could be said to have initiated a new phase of the debate. In this section their work is examined in depth. The emerging criticism of their view – most of which is as yet unpublished – is then evaluated in the section which follows.

In their book, based on a major research project, Charles Kerchner and Douglas Mitchell argue the case for the generational development of teacher unions. Their model, while based purely on research carried out in the United States, may have wider validity. Indeed, as will become apparent, the way in which I have divided up the NUT's history in previous chapters is intended not only to make sense in its own terms, but also to relate closely to the generational model of development advocated by Kerchner and Mitchell.

Teacher unions, like other unions, have a much wider range of functions than simply engaging in collective bargaining on behalf of their members. For many trade unions a long part of their early history is concerned with establishing the right to free collective bargaining. Unions have first to gain the right to organize. Only when that is established can they begin to strive for the right to engage in the collective bargaining process, which leads to binding agreements with the employer. Having achieved that, they may then be in a position to expand the areas in which employees, their members, have a legitimate interest. Such expansion could, for example, take the form of campaigning for industrial democracy, or some other influence over the broader policy-making process. In short, the right to exist precedes the right to bargain, which in turn precedes any right to a broader involvement in policy. These perceptions underpin Kerchner and Mitchell's work.

They argue that the teacher unions in their study of school

districts in California and Illinois are each organized around one of these three core ideas. Because each individual union tends to pass through the first stage on the way to the second and so on, they describe each stage as a generation. 'The essence of each generation', they argue, 'is captured in three common phrases used to describe the relationship between teachers and their employers, the school boards' (Kerchner and Mitchell, 1988, p. 4):

   (i) the 'meet-and-confer' generation;
  (ii) the 'good faith bargaining' generation; and
 (iii) the 'negotiated policy' generation.

Though these are analytically separate, it is possible for them to overlap, so that at a given moment a union might share features of two or more of them.

In passing from one generation to the next, teacher unions and their employers tend to pass through a period of conflict, in which there is a clash of ideologies and sometimes industrial and political upheaval, after which the new order is institutionalized. Labour relations therefore go through a cycle of crisis, institution, accommodation, discontent and crisis again. At the end of each period of crisis, however, neither the union nor the employer is back at square one. On the contrary, they have moved into the next generation. Kerchner and Mitchell put no time limits on the length of either each generation or each 'intergenerational conflict'; of the period of conflict they say it may last anything 'from several weeks to several years'; what defines it is not its length but the extent to which it transforms the relationship between teacher union and employer.

They argue that the vast majority of the school districts in their sample of over one hundred in Illinois and California are in the second generation, 'good faith bargaining'. Each of these had moved through the first generation, 'meet-and-confer', where a handful of the sample firmly remained. Another handful had passed through the 'good faith bargaining' generation and are 'third-generation' unions that 'negotiate policy'. To enable the argument to develop, it is worth examining briefly how Kerchner and Mitchell characterize each of the three generations.

The meet-and-confer generation

In this generation the right of teachers to organize is established. This in itself was a radical demand in its day, as battles across the United States and England and Wales, and no doubt elsewhere, testify. Indeed, in parts of the American South, there are no teacher unions even now. The conflict in Portsmouth in 1896 is a good British example (see Chapter 2). Unions of teachers in particular were seen as suspect by some elements of society, both because of their status as public employees and because of their influence on the minds of future generations. Indeed, traces of this suspicion can be found in the popular press even today. However, the growing status of the teaching profession, and the increased emphasis on its training – evident, for example, in late nineteenth-century England and Wales – gave credibility to the idea of employers consulting with representatives of teachers. Emphasis on the importance of human relations and the value of teachers' expertise in making management decisions reinforced the case.

Consultation is, however, not negotiation: 'Meet-and-confer sessions are predicated on the assumption that both sides are committed to defining and solving mutual problems' (Kerchner and Mitchell, 1988, p. 5). In other words, teachers and their employers have common interests; above all they put pupils first. Indeed, in the first generation, the idea of teachers promoting their own self-interest is often considered somewhat sordid by both teachers and their employers. In this generation, teachers may be consulted across a range of matters, but the rights of the employers to manage and to establish the conditions within which teachers work are not challenged. When they are, conflict ensues; from this the 'good faith bargaining' generation emerges.

The good faith bargaining generation

The core of this generation is that teachers have the right to negotiate their pay and conditions. In contradistinction to the meet-and-confer generation, the underlying assumption is that teachers and their employers have conflicting interests. The role of the negotiation process is to reach agreement, preferably without overt conflict manifested in, for example, strike action. Indeed, conflict management is a key characteristic of the second generation. In addition to formal negotiating machinery, discipline and grievance procedures are developed. Carrying out the often complex procedures correctly becomes a key skill for representatives of both union and management. Relationships focus on agreements, either national or local (or 'the contract' in the United States), and quasi-legal or legal arguments about the meaning of 'the words on the paper' become important. Hence industrial relations can become a highly technical matter which is beyond the immediate grasp of outsiders. Indeed, outsiders such as parents, other members of the community, or even the less active members of the union, if they try to become involved, tend to be viewed as interfering. Meanwhile the participants in the bargaining process often develop a 'cosy' relationship, in which the focus is on reaching agreements that both sides can 'deliver'. The employer must deliver the elected members of the school board or LEA, while the union representative must deliver the members. Negotiators sometimes described this process as being like a tunnel. Employer and employee are approaching each other from opposite ends of the tunnel, but both need the same skills, and where they meet is the key factor.

In short, second-generation teacher unions follow the model of industrial unions, with all its benefits and pitfalls. As a result, they must, consciously or unconsciously, exclude from the bargaining process educational issues which obstinately defy 'industrial definition'. While educational arguments may be deployed in negotiation, direct focus on issues such as the curriculum, or levels of achievement, is excluded from the bargaining process. Such issues may be discussed in a separate consultative forum, but this only serves still further to maintain the artificial distinction between them and matters for negotiation.

Yet all of those involved in the good faith bargaining generation are well aware that their agreements, or lack of them, inevitably affect the quality of educational provision, as are those outside the process. As a consequence, two semi-contradictory influences can begin to undermine second-generation unionism. On the one hand, the process is challenged from outside by people calling for 'accountability' or arguing that 'teachers' or 'the unions' are responsible for the failure of schools. On the other hand, there are those within the unions who argue that their leaders have grown 'too remote' from the members and become 'too cosy' with the employers and too prone to 'selling out'. These are the forces that cause the second inter-generational conflict. Elements of this type of process were evident in the 1980s in England and Wales (see Chapter 5).

The negotiated policy generation

In their sample of over a hundred school districts, Kerchner and Mitchell found very few which had emerged from the second period of inter-generational conflict and become fully fledged third-generation unions. Nevertheless they are able to outline, and indeed advocate, the key features of the third generation.

The first major characteristic is an explicit recognition on all sides that the quality of educational provision cannot be separated from the negotiation process; indeed, it becomes central to it. Hence 'patterns of authority and social interaction [in schools]; the definition of what will be taught, for how long and to whom; and the determination of who has the right to decide how planning, evaluation and supervision of instruction will be carried out' all become legitimate areas for negotiation and resolution (Kerchner and Mitchell, 1988, p. 9). The inclusion of such themes brings about a need for a new form of written agreement, since the concept of 'delivering' on subjects such as these is much more problematic.

Kerchner and Mitchell urge, therefore, that traditional second-generation contracts should be supplemented or replaced by 'Educational Policy Trust Agreements', which, instead of setting out simply to govern behaviour (as ordinary agreements do), would focus on the goals of activity in school. Levels of achievement, educational priorities and 'the rights and obligations of everyone involved in schools' would become legitimate areas for discussion. There would be a mutual recognition that the intended beneficiaries of all that occurred in schools were neither the employer nor the teachers, but the pupils and the wider community. As a result the effectiveness of Educational Policy Trust Agreements would need to be reviewed systematically with all parties involved, and amended as necessary.

In short, the Educational Policy Trust Agreements would provide criteria by which both the success of the education service, and the causes of its success or failure, could be assessed. The explicit recognition of the importance of the goals of the education service would be beneficial. The futile division between pay and conditions on one side and educational issues on the other would, by contrast, be brought to an end. The benefit for the education authority, and the community on whose behalf it exercises power, is a clearer focus on the quality of provision; the benefit for teachers is that only if they are recognized as valued professionals with substantial control over their work can the goals be achieved.

The nature of inter-generational conflict

In addition to explaining in outline what each generation consists of, it is also important to look at what Kerchner and Mitchell identify as central features of inter-generational conflict.

It has already been explained that Kerchner and Mitchell do not believe that duration is crucial to the definition of inter-generational conflict. What defines it, they argue, is whether or not it has structural consequences. Hence, to use British examples, the Durham dispute in the early 1950s was not part of a process which altered the nature of teacher unions or their relations with local or central government and is therefore not part of an inter-generational conflict (see Chapter 4). On the other hand, the Rhondda dispute of 1919 (see Chapter 2) and the national strikes of the mid-1980s (see Chapter 5) clearly were, since both resulted in challenges to the legitimacy of existing structures.

Kerchner and Mitchell also diagnose the symptoms of such conflict. They are often fought around potent symbols or images such as 'choice', 'dignity' or 'accountability'. They can spill over into political conflicts outside the education system, and become perhaps celebrated issues in local or national politics. A struggle for wider popular support is therefore often a feature. They may lead to challenges to, and replacement of, figures of authority on both sides of the conflict. Sir Keith Joseph, the Conservative Secretary of State for Education replaced in 1986 at the height of the dispute, is a classic example. All of this, needless to say, can have devastating effects on a school system, as routines are broken down by the inevitable uncertainty, the changes of leadership and ultimately the altered relationships between teachers and their employers.

It should be emphasized that Kerchner and Mitchell identified these features of conflict on the basis of a study solely of American school districts, and at no time attempt to relate their work either to the United Kingdom or indeed to the national level of any country. Such British examples as have been used, have been introduced partly to assist with explaining the theory to British readers by use of familiar examples, but also to illustrate the point that Kerchner and Mitchell's argument may have relevance to the British experience.

Apart from their important attempt to develop a dynamic view of the development of teacher unions, Kerchner and Mitchell have also undertaken to explore the impact of second-generation teacher unions on the education service. They suggest, however, that teacher unions in either the first or third generation will also have an extensive impact, though of a different nature. They separate out three strands of impact. These are looked at in turn.

Firstly, they analyse the impact on school governance, which as they see it poses two questions; what effect has the growth of teacher unions had on the democratic control of education, and to what extent have they helped or hindered in maintaining public confidence in education? On the latter point, they argue that teacher unions, in the second generation, have been detrimental, an argument which finds echoes in the disputes of the 1970s and 1980s in England and Wales. As regards the unions' impact on the former system, Kerchner and Mitchell maintain that it has been substantial. Indeed, they argue that different forms of democratic control operate at different points in the cycle of conflict between unions and their employers. Though in Britain there have, certainly from the right in the 1980s, been accusations that the educational establishment has resisted the popular will of 'parents', the view barely stands up to the evidence. On the one hand, the demands of parents turn out to be different to those made on their behalf by right-wing politicians; on the other, when a broadly popular view does emerge in education, it is rarely possible for teacher unions to resist it, even if they want to.

The second area Kerchner and Mitchell explore is the impact on school organization. Here they argue that in the second generation the overemphasis on conflict management leads to a neglect of issues of organizational effectiveness. Hence, they point out, a brief strike is seen as a failure, while a long, potentially much more destructive, attritional dispute that does not lead to strike action may be seen as a success. The whole process, they argue, leads also to bureaucratization and formalization of relationships, while decision-making becomes more complex. All this draws 'attention away from establishing a productive organisational culture' (Kerchner and Mitchell, 1988, p. 15). In short, the industrial model of trade unionism proves unable to tackle effectively the issues of educational quality, and indeed, they would argue, causes it to be marginalized.

They attribute most significance, however, to the impact of second-generation teacher unionism on 'the nature of teaching work'. Second-generation unionism, with its emphasis on the industrial model, encourages a view of teaching as labour, with concomitant tendencies 'to direct supervision and to rationalising teaching tasks', at the expense of its potentially professional elements. In addition, they suggest second-generation unionism encourages teachers to see themselves as less professional. Furthermore, they claim their data support the view that 'there is a connection between what teachers do collectively and who they are occupationally' (*ibid.*, p. 18). Those who have watched the profession in this country reeling from the disputes and setbacks of the mid- and late 1980s will surely not disagree entirely with this conclusion.

Professional unionism evaluated

The work of Kerchner and Mitchell has been covered in depth in the previous sections because of its importance in provoking an international academic debate and because it would appear to offer valuable insights into the future of teacher organizations in this country. In this section the emerging critique of their model is unravelled, and then an attempt is made to draw some conclusions appropriate to the British experience.

One of the most aggressive attacks on Kerchner and Mitchell has come from Andrew Spaull of Monash University in Australia, who describes their work as 'a wasted effort' (Spaull, 1990). In his view, Kerchner and Mitchell are recommending to teacher unions a path that subordinates them to management goals. They want, he argues, to turn unions from 'an industrial to a professional mission', which he claims raises 'an obsolete debate'. In particular he believes that what Kerchner and Mitchell do is to attempt to bring teacher unions within the ambit and discourse of modern American human resource management theory; 'their work has the shape and smell of the new industrial relations writing.'

This outburst is, however, an indication of an underlying weakness in Spaull's critique. After all, when a writer stoops to commenting on 'the smell' of a piece of research, it suggests that he or she may have difficulties in commenting on the substance of it. Throughout Spaull's argument what emerges is anger rather than analysis, and as a result, while he hits the target occasionally, much goes astray.

Most teacher unionists would, I suspect, be delighted rather than dismayed by Kerchner and Mitchell's attempt, which Spaull criticizes, 'to find strategies to restore the place of teacher unions in the educational polity'. That is precisely where they belong. Furthermore, what Kerchner and Mitchell do, as I understand it, is not to separate industrial and professional goals, as Spaull claims, but to synthesize them. One need not agree with the precise synthesis they propose for third generation unions, but the aim is surely worthwhile.

Furthermore, Spaull makes no attempt to take account of the nature of management in 1980s America, nor of the social pressures upon it. Like it or not, the school boards in the United States are highly democratic; like it or not, they have been operating for the last decade or so against the background of grave disquiet about the education system. Neither management nor teacher organizations can ignore this background; certainly teacher unions would be failing their members if they did. In these circumstances it is surely valuable to examine the implications of human resource management theory.

That is not to say it should be swallowed whole, and in this Spaull certainly has a point. Spaull is also apposite in pointing out that Kerchner and Mitchell focus too narrowly on teacher unions' relations to management and ignore the unions' multidimensional nature. If they are to develop new means to influence in the next generation, he argues, should they not seek to unionize teachers in places like South Carolina, where they are currently ununionized? Should they not seek unity between different teacher organizations? And should they not build alliances with other trade unions? These are important questions to raise. Spaull provides no evidence that these ideas will work, though that is not to assert there is none. In November 1990 in Massachusetts, for example, a tax roll-back referendum question was heavily defeated by a coalition dominated by the state's trade union movement, and including powerful influence from the Massachusetts Teachers' Association. The Massachusetts experience is not necessarily transferable; a great deal of long-term planning went into the overturning of the proposal, and the state has a powerful liberal tradition.

It should also be noted that Spaull does develop the case for building alliances with the rest of the labour movement, as opposed to Kerchner and Mitchell's professional unionism route. It may be that the two options are not incompatible, a point which will be developed in the final section of this book.

A more considered critique of the Kerchner and Mitchell thesis appears in Martin Lawn's paper, 'Re-inventing the Polite Trade Union?' (1990). This paper is particularly important for the purposes of this chapter, since it sets its argument firmly in the British context. Lawn establishes the threat posed by the 1988 Education Reform Act to teacher organizations. In the new reality, 'the role of teacher organisations is not very clear' (Lawn, 1990). Indeed, he argues that it raises questions about the 'effective existence of teacher unions'. An attempt to answer precisely these questions is made in the concluding section of this book. Nevertheless, it is significant that Lawn implicitly approaches Kerchner and Mitchell as a possible set of answers to these fundamental questions.

Lawn, however, begins by questioning whether their view of generational development applies outside of the USA, where their research was undertaken. This is an important point since a generational, or stage, theory, if it is to be of significance, ought to have applicability across time and space. The historical chapters of this book suggest that Kerchner and Mitchell's work may apply more widely.

While Lawn recognizes that the generational approach has 'some theoretical value', and is 'also a historically accurate notion of unionism and the deep debates over courses of action, allies and politics', he disputes some of the features Kerchner and Mitchell ascribe to it. The shifts from one generation to the next, he says, appear to depend too much on employer rather than union acts. This criticism seems to me to be unfair. To take British examples, it is clear that the crisis at the end of the First World War was generated by changes in both employer and union views and indeed by divisions within both. Kerchner and Mitchell describe precisely this process in their inter-generational conflict.

More substantial is Lawn's view – echoing Spaull – that Kerchner and Mitchell depend to too great an extent on modern American management theory in describing their view of third generation or professional unionism. His view is that the third generation model outlined by Kerchner and Mitchell has more benefits for management than teachers. Management, he argues, gains a flexible task-based workforce which has clear targets and is constantly evaluated. The teachers gain involvement in school-level policy-making, an impact on the scope and character of education policy and greater responsibility for their professional judgements. Which of these represents the most gain is a matter of opinion.

It might be remarked in passing that a proposal which offers such significant gain on both sides is certainly worth considering. However, for Lawn the key is that, under the model, 'management has the last word and so, significantly for the idea of new unionism, it is the unions which may suffer.' This is important; while individual teachers might gain, their organizations may be weakened. The firm ground of collective bargaining is threatened, and the workplace teams may cut across traditional school-level influence.

Certainly this has happened in some parts of industry where human resource management has been applied. As we shall see in the next section, some of the changes affecting the education service in England and Wales present teacher unions with this challenge and therefore have major implications for the way in which they operate. The key to their success will be rapid, effective support for members in schools; a supply of quality advice on educational and professional as well as traditional trade union issues; and consistent, effective advocacy on behalf of teachers at national level, where policy will continue to be made. In addition, teacher unions will need the power – albeit normally held in reserve – to say 'no' when it matters, and mean it.

Lawn's argument that Kerchner and Mitchell fail to take significant account of the influence on conflict of factors outside the education service is also important. As Lawn's own research has shown, the wave of radicalism in the wider trade union movement was central to the thinking of activists such as W.G. Cove in the aftermath of the First World War. Broad political strategy was also clearly in the minds of H.A.L. Fisher and his colleagues in the government during the same period. Similarly, in the 1980s, the teachers' pay dispute can only be understood, as we have seen, as part of a wider conflict between the government and trade unions, particularly in the public sector. The Kerchner and Mitchell thesis on inter-generational conflict needs re-examination or at least further work in the light of this case. To what extent did external factors affect the timing and nature of the inter-generational conflict in their research sample?

An important addition to this aspect of Lawn's critique is that the state as a political concept is absent from the Kerchner and Mitchell analysis. This is perhaps understandable in a study of so localized an education system as that of the United States, but if the thesis is to be in any sense international, it will need to be taken into account. As Lawn points out, teachers are state employees with a degree of obligation to democratically established priorities. Their training is the subject of state regulation, as the 1989 CATE criteria illustrate. Even in the United States recently we have seen, at both state and federal level, a high level of concern about educational issues and attempts to direct policy. As Lawn correctly asserts, 'the more centralised and overt the control over teachers, the more likely they will engage in political campaigns with opposition groups to counter state influence.'

Overall, Lawn's critique of Kerchner and Mitchell provides a challenge to their approach which, in my view, will require at least a modification. If their views are to be in any sense internationally applicable (and it should be stressed they have never claimed they are), they may need a more substantial revision. None of this reduces the importance of Kerchner and Mitchell's work as a major step forward in thinking about teacher unions. The debate which they have begun will undoubtedly bear fruit. Moreover, as the next section will reveal, their ideas may provide the raw material for a strategy for teacher unions, at least in England and Wales, into the next century.

The effects of reform 1988–91

The traditional post-war strength of the NUT was based on its large membership, which included over half the teaching profession into the 1970s and 1980s and 40 per cent or more until the present time. This gave it majorities in the teachers' panels of the key negotiating committees such as Burnham and CLEA/ST, as well as some legitimacy for claiming to represent the teaching force as a whole. With all of this came status. As a result, the NUT was able to influence powerfully the course of negotiation, and indeed to originate the claims made on behalf of all teachers. In fact, through much of the post-war period the NUT worked hard to accommodate the views of other teacher organizations; but the decision to do so (or not) was in its hands. This power gave it a membership attraction, particularly for those keen to be active in teacher unionism, which the other teacher organizations could not match. It also brought it recognition from the other players in educational politics, including the government at both national and local level.

As a result it had extensive influence in the educational policy-making process. Its role in organizations such as the Schools' Council has already been referred to in Chapter 5.

Importantly, the NUT was also extremely influential at LEA

level, in both negotiation and policy formation. In local negotiating bodies the NUT normally had a majority on the teachers'
side paralleling its representation in national bodies. It therefore
tended to lead the way in local negotiations. The NUT Div-
isional Secretary, supported by briefing material from headquarters, was a key powerbroker at LEA level, in a way in which
equivalents in other teacher organizations were not. The pattern
of local committees varies: in some LEAs there is a joint negotiating committee (JNC), others have a joint consultative committee (JCC), and a substantial number have both. JNCs tend to
have a more formal negotiating role; JCCs a more widely rang-
ing agenda covering educational issues (Matthews, 1989). In
addition to its influence through negotiation and consultation,
teacher representation on LEA education committees provided
the NUT with an opportunity to impact directly on the democratic decision-making forum. Much of this local network of
influence remains in place; indeed this paragraph could have
been written in the present tense but, perhaps, for the steadily
growing influence of the Education Reform Act.

Finally, the NUT had influence at school level through its
school representatives; on health and safety issues, for example.
Across from 20,000 to 30,000 schools in England and Wales,
the effectiveness of school representatives is obviously variable.
Nevertheless, they have formed, until recently, the main channel
of membership recruitment and of communication to less active
or non-active members. Indeed, in spite of direct mailing of
information to members and the centralization of subscriptions
collection, the school representative remains the human face of
the Union for most members.

The reforms of the late 1980s, which flow from the 1987
Teachers' Pay and Conditions Act and the 1988 Education
Reform Act, challenge each aspect of this structure of union
influence. We now turn to examine the impact of those legisla-
tive changes. It is important to see how the various elements
relate to each other in their impact on teachers and their unions.

Until 1987, the levels of teachers' pay and the salary structure were nationally negotiated in the Burnham Committee, and its agreements had statutory force. Conditions of service were negotiated nationally in CLEA/ST with representatives of local authorities, and applied across England and Wales. Since then the picture has changed radically, and is continuing to change. The withdrawal of teachers' negotiating rights in 1987 and the imposition of successive pay and conditions settlements through the Interim Advisory Committee (IAC) in the years since then have radically altered the pay structure.

At a popular level the focus has been on the level of pay awards. In the long run, however, it is likely that the growing flexibility in the pay levels of individual teachers will be perceived to be the most significant development of the IAC era. The IAC flexibility recommendations have introduced the possibility of awarding teachers extra increments or inter-incremental payments not only for additional responsibility, but also for their performance in the classroom or to assist in the retention of teachers in shortage subjects. The 1991 IAC Report gives the power over each of these elements of flexibility to the governing bodies of schools (DES, 1991).

These recommendations need to be seen in the broader context of the implementation of local management of schools (LMS). This aspect of the 1988 Education Reform Act, which gives governors control of schools' budgets, including the staffing budget, has already been implemented in virtually all secondary schools and many primary schools. It will soon be in place in every school including, in a modified form, special schools. As a result, it will be necessary for every school to have its own pay policy. The level of an individual teacher's pay will therefore be in the hands of school governors in a way it has not been since the First World War. Governors will need to decide, if they have not already, what their policy is on the elements of pay flexibility. They may in most cases simply implement advice provided by LEAs, but they are not required to. The early evidence suggests that, on the recommendation of the unions, most governing bodies have made little use of pay flexibility, but this is unlikely to remain the case permanently. This represents a revolution in Burnham terms.

The revolution is due to go further still. The proposed Review Body which, unlike other similar bodies, would control both pay and conditions, can be expected to recommend extending flexibility still further in both pay and conditions, while promoting the idea of performance-related pay. Furthermore, its recommendations would not apply to grant-maintained schools. Some grant-maintained schools are following in the footsteps of city technology colleges, some of which have already moved in the direction of not only individual contracts but also non-recognition of teacher unions. As Martin Lawn has pointed out (Lawn, 1990), from a union point of view this raises the spectre of 'sweetheart deals', 'single union' deals, or even teachers on individual contracts. A group of Conservative backbenchers was reported in January 1991 to have urged Kenneth Clarke to aim for a teaching force with each teacher on an individual contract.

If all of this is likely to threaten severely the traditional national negotiating strength of the NUT, there are also threats to its local power base. As we have seen, in the last decade LEAs have been under fire almost as much as teachers have. They have lost some powers – such as that over the curriculum – to the centre, and others – particularly resource allocation and personnel powers – to schools. They have also been financially squeezed. They are therefore becoming less able to'deliver' on a range of matters of importance to a teacher union. Whereas in the past they could require a school to accept a redeployed teacher, they are no longer able to. They normally also had the option of adding a teacher no longer needed in a particular school to the LEA's support staff. The requirement under LMS to minimize the element of the education budget held centrally by the LEA makes this virtually impossible. As a result, redundancies have begun to occur where in the past they did not. On a range of other issues of importance to the unions, LEAs have had to resort to issuing advice to governors where previously the decision was in their hands. Equal opportunities appointments procedure is one example among many.

This does not make the LEA powerless, however. Advice for governors, such as that issued by Hampshire on personnel matters, has often been negotiated at LEA level within the unions and then welcomed in schools (Hampshire LEA, 1990). Chief Education Officers have the right to be involved in appointments, and can use this right assertively. LEAs also have responsibilities in relation to curriculum and assessment, through which they can influence schools. In addition, grants for in-service education, and the obligation to ensure teachers are appraised, are in their hands.

A teacher union must therefore continue to seek to represent its members powerfully at LEA level in spite of the reduced ability of the LEA to 'deliver'. Since this has been a traditional strength of the NUT, and sometimes other unions, maintaining it is relatively straightforward. The problem is the growing need for simultaneous union influence at school level. Successful advocacy in 116 LEAs is one thing; supporting it in 24,000 schools is quite another. Yet, as governors begin to exercise their personnel powers – discipline and dismissal included – and operate the pay flexibility already at their disposal, this is the challenge facing the NUT and the other teacher organizations.

The government's determined destruction of the partnership policy-making model has emphasized the need to win support at school level not only from teachers but from parents and governors too (see Chapter 5). As we have seen, this has necessitated an approach to influencing policy through winning public support rather than direct influence in smoke-filled rooms. Tellingly, in its *National Curriculum Newsletter* number 6 (NUT, September 1991), the Union argued 'For, if one effect of the Education Reform Act is excessive centralization, the other, unexpected by government perhaps, is that a school in which parents, governors and teachers work together is virtually invincible.'

It is important to recognize that this analysis broadly applies regardless of the outcome of the next general election. A future

Labour government, as has been made abundantly clear, would develop and implement policy more independently of the trade unions than previous Labour governments have done. A Labour Secretary of State for Education would also retain many of the extensive range of powers which that office acquired under the 1988 Education Reform Act. Furthermore, the education policy of a future Labour government would emphasize accountability to parents and leave a reformed LMS System in place, with governors therefore retaining extensive powers. It must be anticipated that extensive flexibility would remain with governors in relation to pay.

This is not to say that there would be no difference. On the contrary, the differences would be stark. Labour rejects the market model and is committed to resolving the anomalies under the current scheme of LMS which give the powers of employers to governing bodies, while leaving the LEAs with the responsibilities. A Labour government would also return grant-maintained schools and city technology colleges to LEA control; this would bring to an end potential threats to union recognition and collective bargaining. Furthermore, it can be anticipated that the government money, in excess of £80 million, currently used to subsidize the independent schools sector through the Assisted Places Scheme, would be redirected into the state sector. There is also a commitment to increasing expenditure on education over the lifetime of a parliament.

Labour has also promised to establish a General Teachers' Council. Such a body would provide teachers with a national voice on professional issues, though it would have no involvement in the issues of pay and conditions. It might contribute to unifying teachers' views on the future of the education service. The danger would be that in order to mask the genuine differences about policy direction between groups of teachers, the General Teachers' Council would be able to promote only the bland or the obvious. The extent of agreement between teacher organizations in 1990 and 1991 on issues such as testing and teacher appraisal suggests, however, that more promising outcomes would be likely. If so, it would further encourage teacher unions to think long term about education policy, and to enhance their status and pay by convincing the public of the need for high-quality education in every school.

These Labour Party commitments, if implemented, would no doubt be broadly welcomed by the NUT and probably by the other teacher organizations. They would not, however, obviate the need for the teacher unions to seek alternative means of influencing the course of events in the 1990s. The power structures of the 1970s would not be restored.

In short, the outcome of the next election will not alter the need for teacher unions to re-appraise their strategy radically.

All of this has radical implications for union organization, tactics and strategy. The challenge to a union is how to continue to defend and promote members' interests in the aftermath of an attack which has broken or impaired many traditional means of influence. The final section of this book is devoted to bringing together the analysis of power set out in the previous chapter, the lessons of the debate about a new teacher unionism, and the implications of recent government legislation; and through that process drawing some tentative conclusions about a teacher union strategy for the 1990s. The prospects in my view – perhaps perversely – are optimistic.

The strategic union

The crisis of the 1980s – what Kerchner and Mitchell might have termed the second inter-generational conflict – is incomplete. As a result, power relationships within the education system remain, in many respects, fluid and uncertain. In such circumstances there are opportunities for organizations that think boldly and creatively to take advantage of the opportunities. However, they need to avoid simply being buffetted in whichever direction the wind happens to be blowing and ensure that they head for a destination of their choosing, however distant it might appear to be.

In circumstances such as those facing the NUT at the start of the 1990s – an uncertain present having followed a highly influential past – the temptation is to see turning the clock back as the chief policy goal. It would assist the Union if LEAs were given back their personnel powers; it would strengthen the Union if its influence in national bargaining was restored; its policy influence would be rebuilt if organizations such as the Schools' Council were re-established. There are, however, three major problems with setting such goals.

Firstly, they are politically unrealistic; there is no party at national level advocating such a programme, presumably because each of the parties – probably rightly – believes that it would be unpopular. Secondly, and perhaps more fundamentally, it is important to recognize that the demands made on the education service have changed significantly. Increasingly, the economic imperatives – the changing nature of work and technology, for example – will require an education system in which all young people leave school with a sense of achievement. Yet the pre-1980s model consistently failed almost half of the school population. In short, even if it were politically achievable, it would be educationally undesirable.

The third reason for rejecting a turning back of the clock is that the opportunities opening up could enable the NUT, and perhaps other teacher organizations, to achieve an influence greater than, though radically different from, that which it held in the past. There are three trends working in favour of teacher unions which they need to exploit, and which have been touched on already in the Introduction.

Firstly, the growing demands of the economy for a highly skilled, flexible workforce made up of individuals able to think innovatively, and to work collaboratively in teams, will increasingly require an education system which is seen as an investment, and which concentrates on ensuring achievement for all pupils. This coincides with the views that teachers and the NUT have promoted on principle for years.

Secondly, there is the change in understanding of management structures, with participative, flatter models increasingly being seen as more effective. As this trend begins to influence the education service (and it is already doing so: the *Times Educational Supplement* of 25 January 1991 contained the headline, 'Flattening out the hierarchy' above an article which dealt with precisely this issue), there will be opportunities for teacher influence in school management that have not been available in the past.

Thirdly, there is the increasing evidence that the government's market model of education is simply not going to work. The constant alterations of the curriculum and assessment proposals; the growing disaster of teacher shortage, turnover and morale; and the increasing contrast between schools in wealthy areas and those in poor districts could be cited as evidence of their failure. Teacher shortage itself is of course a powerful lever for the unions, and growing political and economic concern about the role of women in the workforce can be turned to the advantage of a profession which in numbers, if not yet in influence, is predominantly female.

None of these makes the success of teacher unions inevitable. They all, however, open up room for manoeuvre and opportunities for them to exploit. Whether the NUT will do so depends on decisions taken by members and their representatives in the years ahead. What is certain, however, is that, in spite of the pressures the NUT and its rivals have been put under in the 1980s, they are still an influential force, and there are growing opportunities for them to begin to build that influence.

With a contradictory combination of boldness and doubt, the rest of this chapter is designed to provide an outline sketch of a model of teacher unionism suited to the conditions of the decade ahead. As a title for the model I reject the Kerchner and Mitchell proposal of 'professional unionism', for two reasons. Firstly, the term 'professional' has, as Martin Lawn above all has shown, been powerfully contested during this century and is therefore open to misinterpretation. Secondly, perhaps because it has been contested, it has too conservative a ring and content to it and the times seem to me to demand a radical approach. I have chosen in preference, therefore, the title 'strategic unionism' for reasons which should become clear.

Vision

Trade unionists know that success in negotiations usually comes from having clear objectives and sticking to them, whatever distractions might arise. This process might not give you all you set out to achieve, but it is more successful than entering negotiations and waiting to see what turns up.

This analogy is relevant to the strategic and long-term goals of any organization. It is particularly important in a period of uncertainty and fluid power relationships. Strategic thinking is therefore a prerequisite of success for a teacher union in the 1990s. Teacher unions will need a long-term vision of the changes they would like to see brought about and a cogent strategy for moving towards this vision. In business jargon this is called a mission statement.

To be effective it must be more than words on paper. It must be based on an analysis of what is possible, and it must generate the support and commitment of the union's members and its staff. As a Swedish trade unionist said to a visiting Australian delegation recently:

> Unions must have a long-range strategy based on careful analysis.
> Without such a strategy unions are confined to being reactive to the initiatives of others. They cannot then fully participate in setting the national agenda nor can they even adequately pursue the interests of their members, much less the interests of the wider community.
> The overall strategy needs to be widely debated, widely understood and widely supported by the membership. (quoted in NUT, 1990b, p. 169)

While in any democratic organization, and certainly within the NUT historically, there have been many policy controversies, broad consensus is by no means unachievable. The Union's long-term curriculum policy, *A Strategy for the Curriculum* (NUT, 1990a), received the unanimous support of the Executive and has been widely acclaimed by the membership. It represented a conscious attempt by the Union to move into a strategic mode of policy thinking. It represents, perhaps more than any other policy statement to date, the kind of thinking that the Swedish trade unionist was advocating, and that is required by teacher unions in the UK in the 1990s.

I have argued elsewhere the reasons for strategic thinking in relation to the curriculum. While not entirely transferable to all policy areas, the argument is worth quoting at length:

> There are several reasons why it is important for teachers' organisations to take this step. For a start, it is already clear that the National Curriculum, as conceived by those who framed the Education Reform Act, lacks coherence, is riddled with contradiction, cannot be implemented without a series of substantial modifications and, most seriously of all, cannot conceivably meet the challenge of education in the 1990s. There is therefore an urgent need for coherent proposals to be put forward in an attempt to generate debate and hopefully, as a result, consensus.
>
> Secondly, the responses to the government proposals so far have tended to be pragmatic and have in any case always left the government in control of the agenda. In other words, debate about the curriculum ... has been for or against the National Curriculum, and not about what the education challenge of the 21st century consists of and the various possible models of the curriculum that would enable the education system to meet that challenge.
>
> The implication of developments such as the process of internationalisation, increasing EC unity, the expansion of democracy on a global scale, and the changing nature of work and leisure are considered not as serious curriculum questions requiring answers, but as technical problems about how they can be squeezed into the inflexible, overburdened, subject-based National Curriculum framework. By setting out a genuine and hopefully popular alternative – and the response so far indicates a widespread welcome – the NUT hopes to open up these questions for serious debate.
>
> Thirdly, by having a coherent alternative, the NUT is in a position

to respond consistently to government proposals over a period of time. Given the range of pressures on teachers' unions and the rapidly changing political context in which they operate, it is all too easy to respond to educational questions on the basis of short-term tactical considerations. For example, some teachers' representatives have opposed the idea of Records of Achievement, not on the basis of their educational merits, but because of the current excessive workload on teachers. While this is an understandable reaction in the circumstances, a series of such responses in the long run enables opponents of the unions to portray them as negative, opposed to positive change, and as barriers to the development of quality education.

The need to avoid precisely this uncomfortable corner provides the fourth and final justification for moving into a strategic phase of educational thinking. In the era of corporatist policy-making, the NUT was able to influence government decision directly. During Ronald Gould's term as General Secretary (1946–70) he had access to the minister and to the powerful national representatives of the LEAs. In addition, NUT officials were in regular and routine contact with civil servants in the DES and their equivalents at local level. This model of policy-making made public conflict, and therefore the need to influence public opinion, less important. With the break-up of the partnership and the conscious attempt on the part of the government to exclude teacher unions from the decision-making process, there has been a corresponding increase in the need for the Union to win its educational battles on the board public terrain. The alternative is marginalisation, a union which provides services such as insurance to members but which ceases to be a significant actor in the development of educational policy. In this context, the need for consistency in policy advocacy becomes all-important. Most important of all, it becomes essential for the union to be associated consistently with the promotion of educational quality. *A Strategy for the Curriculum* [NUT, 1990a] is the central element in the NUT's attempt to meet this prescription. Hence, the basis of its argument is not that the present National Curriculum is worse than what preceded it, nor that it is ill-thought-out, nor even that it is being shoddily and hastily implemented, though some or all of these points may be true. It is that the model proposed by the

NUT is better designed to meet the needs of young people and society as we approach the new millennium. (Barber, 1992)

Much of this argument would apply across all of the Union's work and requires a disciplined and creative approach to policy-making. As we have seen, successful implementation of strategic thinking would inevitably involve this sort of trade-off between the short and long term. However, unless priority is given to the longer-term strategic goals, the Union is bound to remain an essentially reactive organization, which in the context of the 1990s would be confined to a role on the sidelines of policy development.

Having established the need for a mission statement, the obvious next question is to ask what it might say. This could be avoided by arguing that its drafting needs to be a collaborative process. Nevertheless, it may be of interest to suggest a few items for inclusion, if for no reason other than to generate debate.

A teacher union like the NUT exists to defend and promote the interests of its members. Historically the NUT has taken the view that to do this effectively requires not only working for the salaries and conditions of service of members, but also promoting high quality, publicly provided education for all pupils. Hence it was demanding – for example – secondary education for all some fifty years before this became a reality. The involvement of the Union in these broader issues of education policy has not been a soft distraction from its main task. On the contrary, the historical record shows that Union success in these wider questions can lead to improved salaries and working conditions. At a time when there is a greater need than ever to generate public support for investment in education, the Union's policy advocacy should be a central feature of its work.

At its Harrogate Conference in 1988, the Union confirmed that 'the defence of state education' was, along with the protection of members, a central goal. Its vision should build on this and include:

(i) the promotion of high-quality, publicly provided education;

(ii) an overt commitment to equal opportunities for all pupils;

(iii) a commitment to building close relationships between schools and the community, and to the view that teachers have an accountability to the communities in which they work;

(iv) the promotion of the view that educational achievement for all pupils will depend upon the quality of the teaching profession, and upon ensuring that teachers have the professional space in which to exercise their skills creatively;

(v) the involvement of teachers in decision-making at school and all other levels; and

(vi) a demand for salaries and conditions of service appropriate to the importance of the teachers' role in the education service, and indeed in society generally.

This list is tentative, but would seem to me to chime in both with the NUT's historic role and with the nature of the challenge of the 1990s. Some of the points in this list are developed further in what follows.

Accountability and the community

It has been argued that, as a result of the crisis of the 1980s, it has become essential for a teacher union to win public support for its views as a means of influencing policy. Ultimately, in a democracy, investment in education and the teaching profession will only occur if there is a public demand – either latent or otherwise – for it. It has also been argued that the NUT must begin to compete with government in what Lukes called the third dimension of power; influencing people's perceptions of what they should demand from government.

The problem for the Union in this crucial dimension of power is that people's images of teachers are created not solely by the Union's efforts, but also by a range of other influences, including both the inaccurate or outdated memories adults often have of school, and the day-to-day contact parents have with their children's schools.

The Union must begin to address these aspects of influencing public opinion. Publicity material for parents and governors will be one way of doing so. More effective in the long run, however, will be a confidence among teachers that what they do in schools is of high quality, so that parents and other members of the community are welcomed in.

The traditional defensiveness needs to be, and in some places already has been, swept aside. Most people most of the time are greatly impressed by what happens in schools when they see it for themselves. Everyone who is so impressed becomes that much more likely to be an advocate of the kind of policy the NUT is pursuing. Tactical errors such as refusing to participate in parents' evenings, as happened in the mid-1980s, must be avoided. A consistent approach at school level to winning parental and community support, allied to sophisticated national public relations work (discussed in the last chapter), involving advertising, would be powerful to an extent that neither approach alone could achieve.

Whether LEAs will have a central role in the 1990s model of accountability depends on the 1992 election result. If LEAs regain some confidence and a creative role, they could be highly influential. A partnership between parents, teachers and LEA could work towards agreements on targets for the education service both in terms of levels of achievement and levels of investment. These would be similar to the Educational Policy Trust Agreements advocated by Kerchner and Mitchell (see p. 103). If, on the other hand, the election is followed by further emasculation of LEAs, it is unlikely that they could make such a significant contribution.

To achieve the kinds of link with parents, the community and employers that will have an impact on government policy, teacher unions need to recognize the legitimacy in a democracy of demands for teachers to be accountable. This does not mean accepting the model of accountability to the market which lies behind the Education Reform Act. Indeed, that must be resisted because it conflicts with the Union's commitment to, and the community's need for, high-quality education for all. It does mean recognizing that the extent of professional control – and hence the exclusion of others – that existed in the post-war period over, for example, the curriculum meant that teachers were vulnerable to the attacks of a populist government in the 1980s. Looking back, it can be seen that the decision to concede curriculum control to teachers was in part a result of the fears caused by fascist interference in what was taught in Europe in the inter-war years. Once those anxieties receded, the lack of any theoretical justification for teacher control became apparent.

A balance needs now to be struck. In a democracy, those who have influence – as teachers clearly do – ought to be accountable for it. On the other hand, if accountability is narrowly defined or becomes constricting, then educational quality becomes impossible. Quality in education requires recognition of the skilled, complex, creative and professional nature of teaching; teachers must therefore have considerable control over their work, and space in which to be creative. Quality also results from a sharing between teachers and parents of the aims of education; for this reason teachers need to balance their own aspirations with those of the community in which they serve. The balance in the 1970s and 1980s was not ideal; the Education Reform Act, far from correcting it, has upset it still further. There is a major task here for policy-makers including the teacher unions in the 1990s.

The importance of this argument for teacher unions should not be missed, for its strategic implication is that, by conceding legitimate levels of accountability, unions would put the quality of education at the heart of their mission. This would surely assist in enhancing their relations with the public and hence extend their influence over the policy-making process, thus leading to improved salaries and conditions of service for members.

Responsiveness to members

The traditional power structure with tight national bargaining and powerful influence at LEA level enabled the NUT to represent its members' interests without needing, most of the time, to be directly in touch with them. The break-up of those power structures changes that. Many of the decisions affecting teachers' work and their futures will now be taken at school level. This means that there will be many more individual, school-level demands for support from the Union. Simultaneously, the need for the Union to win its policy goals through effective public relations means informing, consulting and generating commitment from members in a way that was not necessarily done in the past, except perhaps during major disputes. The pace and extent of change also generates a need among members for clear advice. For all these reasons – not to mention the competition between teacher unions for teachers' allegiance – the NUT will need to be highly responsive to its members' needs both collectively and individually.

To some extent the NUT has already begun to respond to these demands. The establishment since 1988 of an expanded regional structure was in anticipation of a growing demand for support of members resulting from the Education Reform Act. Its legal service relates directly to this structure. The establishment of a central record of members' addresses has enabled the Union to distribute its journal, *The Teacher*, into members' homes, thus providing the first direct form of communication between the Union and individual members.

This agenda may need to be advanced further. In addition to the vital democratic structure which is responsible for policy development, it is important that the full-time staff of the Union understand, and are in touch with, the demands and needs of members in schools. Only in this way can the speed and quality of response reach the levels that are likely to be required in a period of probably continuous rapid change.

It will not be adequate, or economic, to respond to members only as casework when there is a problem. As in medicine, prevention is preferable to cure. To satisfy this, the NUT – and its rivals – will no doubt increasingly need to attempt to provide advice – on issues of education, equality, law and conditions of service, for example – that meets members' needs or, better still, anticipates them. In a rapidly changing scene this requires a highly sensitive response mechanism and, again, speed.

To ensure that the needs of members at school level are met effectively will require, too, increasing support for the Union's representatives in schools. The Regional Office network of the NUT is intended to do this, but the representatives will need training and supportive advice across all policy areas too. Given the powers of governors and the lack of flexibility in school budgets, ensuring a continuing supply of volunteers to act as lay officers for the Union – with the right to the time off that union duties require – will be a major organizational problem for the 1990s. There is unlikely to be a simple solution to the problem, but a widespread perception of the Union's success in influencing development at all levels is likely to be the best way of generating commitment.

Training for members in carrying out their Union duties has long been a service offered by the NUT, which has its own training centre. A recent series of courses for teacher governors is an indication of the Union's growing awareness of the need for its members to become influential at school level.

A second aspect of training that the Union has begun to explore is the provision for members of professional education. In 1990, courses on the implications of the Education Reform Act for groups of teachers as teachers (as opposed to teachers as trade unionists) were held. They had two advantages over the training teachers had received from their LEAs on the same issues. Firstly, they provided an up-to-date national perspective and involved teachers meeting others from elsewhere in the country. Secondly, they could provide the kind of critical perspective that those responsible for implementing the changes are unable to do. For the Union at national level they had advantages too; they provided a route for members' views to feed back directly to headquarters. More importantly, they moved the Union into a vacuum which, if it does not fill, others will. Changes in the funding of INSET, with much of the money in the hands of schools, have opened up the INSET market to a range of independent providers, including a growing band of educational consultants. If the Union can find its way into this opening it can weave itself into the fabric of policy development and implementation in a way that will not only assist members, but also add significantly to its policy influence.

There are other ways in which the Union can provide services and thus gain influence in education. Training of non-teacher governors, for example, might not only generate income, but also help to ensure that there are governors who understand teachers' aspirations, and add to the Union's influence. A teacher union like the NUT, among many other things, is a concentration of expertise. In the unformed power structures of the 1990s – and they are likely to remain unformed for some years to come – this expertise can be put to use in a number of different ways. If it is not, others – educational consultants and existing international consultancies such as Coopers Lybrand Deloitte – whose goal is private profit, not the defence and promotion of the teaching profession, will continue to move into the vacuum that has existed and is being rapidly filled.

Finally, of course, the Union, like its counterparts, will need to continue to provide the growing range of membership benefits – insurance, discounts on various services and so on – which have become such a feature of trade unions in the 1980s. However, these should be seen as what they are: fringe benefits; they will never become the *raison d'être* of a teacher union. If unions fail in their chief goals they will never be saved by the offer of a cheap breakdown service.

The strength to say 'no'
There will no doubt be times in the future, however successful the Union is in winning public support, achieving influence and defending members in the new circumstances, when proposals are unacceptable to the mass of the membership. The Union, indeed any serious union, needs to maintain the organizational strength to resist such proposals effectively. This strength is a major reason why people join unions.

How any such proposals should be resisted would depend both on their nature and on a range of tactical questions at the time. There are always different options available; as we have seen in Chapter 6, these range from campaigning activity through to various forms of industrial action, including strike action.

It is difficult to anticipate what sorts of issue might require such resistance, but some hazardous speculation might illustrate the point. Questions regarding the recognition of the Union or, beyond that, the right of a teacher to belong to a particular union would undoubtedly require an effective response. A decade ago recognition would not have been on the agenda, but as an earlier part of the chapter explains, it is by no means unthinkable in the present climate. A mechanistic system of appraisal linked directly to dismissal or discipline might also evoke firm resistance. It might be speculated too that, had the government attempted to impose again on all primary schools the kind of assessment enforced in 1991, it would simply not have been implemented. On a micro-scale, the appointment of a 19-year-old school-leaver to teach geography in a Hertfordshire school in September 1991 clearly undermined the NUT's view of teaching as a profession. A rapid and firm response by the Union led to a complete retreat by the school.

The nature of an organization required to resist effectively could be the subject of another book. It certainly involves effective representation of the Union at all levels of power, high-quality legal advice, skilled and assertive lay and professional officers, considerable financial reserves, good communications internally, excellent public relations work and the commitment throughout the organization to weather a storm. Bloody-mindedness becomes a positive asset at times.

Unity or collaboration
One of the bugbears of teachers and education watchers is the division of the profession in England and Wales into six teacher organizations; and that does not include the teachers in unversities or further and higher education. The divisions have

at times in the recent past been exploited by teachers' opponents and weakened their cause dramatically, most notably during the pay dispute of the mid-1980s. It is clear too that competition and conflict between teacher unions diverts energy and resources, and damages the public image of teachers.

The options for solving the problem include: mergers; the triumph of one union over another in a competitive market (which seems unlikely but is not impossible, as the Scottish experience shows); increasing collaboration on specific issues; or possibly the creation of a General Teachers' Council (GTC). The last of these might assist in presenting a united front on professional issues, but would not deal with pay or conditions. On many issues the need of a GTC to achieve consensus might lead to anodyne statements, but with respect to training, entry standards and professional discipline it might become highly influential. It ought, in any case, to be able to assist in raising the status of teachers as the Engineering Council has done for those in its field.

Collaboration is an increasing feature of the teacher organization world. The unions have been able to make joint statements on a range of issues including ones as controversial as teacher appraisal in the past year or so. At the end of January 1991, very firm and far from anodyne joint advice on pupil assessment and teacher workload was issued by all six. This represented a major step forward in the education policy field and might open up future possibilities. The joint union surveys of teacher shortages in 1989 and 1990 are also examples of successful collaboration.

Whichever of these options for closer unity finds favour, and they are not necessarily mutually exclusive, it is unlikely that the divisions that dogged the 1980s will remain in place to the same extent by the end of the 1990s. If they do, the profession is unlikely to have made the most of the opportunities the 1990s present.

Teacher unions and democracy

In the analysis of power in Chapter 6, it was argued that teacher unions would need in the 1990s to begin to compete effectively in what Lukes describes as the third dimension of power. Much of the present chapter has been concerned with the ways in which a teacher union might be effective in all three dimensions in the 1990s.

There was, however, a second aspect of the third dimension of power which has not yet featured in this discussion, but is potentially the most important of all; namely, the possibility that the party in power, through its control of the education system, might manipulate the curriculum for its own benefit. This fear was, as we have seen, very real in the immediate aftermath of the Second World War.

The health of a democracy depends to some extent on ensuring that manipulation of this kind does not occur. This requires that the education system has sufficient checks and balances within it to ensure that it does not occur. Democracy depends not only on elections, but also on diffuse power structures which limit the possibility of elective dictatorship. The 1944 Education Act and the way in which it was implemented provided the necessary checks and balances; indeed it could be argued that it restricted central government's influence excessively. The 1986 Act dealt with the problem of teachers exploiting the curriculum for political ends – for which there was, incidentally, no evidence – by insisting that politically controversial issues were dealt with in a balanced way. In the 1988 Act, which massively centralized control of the curriculum, there is no section which limits the government or its curriculum policy-makers in the same way. Throughout the development of the National Curriculum there have been fears of overt, even blatant, political interference in the curriculum, most notably in relation to history, but also to some extent in geography and English. The appointment of political confidantes of the government, like John Marks, to the NCC and the SEAC in August 1990 further raised those fears. The 'July coups' at NCC and SEAC in 1991, when two close political allies of the government and staunch Thatcherites, David Pascall and Brian Griffiths, were appointed to chair them, exacerbated anxiety.

Whether these appointments remain within the boundaries of what is acceptable in a democracy is a moot point. The more serious problem is that the structure which the government has created for curriculum control under the 1988 Act destroys or weakens many of the checks and balances that previously existed. As a result, whether the government intervenes excessively or not depends largely on its good will. Since the good will of this or future governments cannot be assumed, this represents a major weakness in the education system. Successful democracy after all depends to some extent on a healthy mistrust of those who hold power.

A glance at the influence under the Education Reform Act of those who used to exercise curriculum control bears out this analysis. Local government's influence has been eroded by the loss of both curricular power to the centre and financial control to the periphery. It is likely to have a support-and-evaluation role in the future, rather than a direct influence on the nature of the curriculum. It has in any case been severely weakened by financial restriction and lives in the shadow of threats of further reorganization, or even its own effective disappearance. The proposal effectively to privatize LEA advisory and inspection services, made by Kenneth Clarke in September 1991, is evidence of the direction of policy as long as the Conservative government remains in power. The LEA, therefore, cannot any longer be seen as an effective check on central government's curriculum control.

Parents and governors, ostensibly the beneficiaries of the recent reforms, also have, in any formal sense, only limited powers over the curriculum. Their main power is one of appeal if a school deviates from the central-government-prescribed curriculum; they cannot appeal against that curriculum. Furthermore, at the moment, it remains to be seen whether parents and governors can find means of expressing their demands effectively in a collective way. If they do not, as they have not done to date, they too are unlikely to be able to check central government's power over the curriculum, though they might be more influential in an individual school. As we have seen, there is potential in alliance at school level of parents, governors and teachers.

At the centre, curriculum power rests with the NCC and SEAC. The Councils both consists entirely of ministerial appointees, who can be changed at will. They are therefore unlikely to provide any significant check on government influence either. Their role is in any case equivocal, since their existing influence depends not only on ministerial appointment but also on maintaining extensive central control of what is taught.

The only remaining factor in the system is teachers. Given the relative weakness of all the other actors in the drama, it falls to teachers to limit government interference. They have a certain amount of power as individuals or as small, school-level groups, but at that level their influence is severely limited by requirements for heads and LEAs to see that the National Curriculum is implemented, and by parental rights of appeal. Their influence will be further limited by imposed standardized assessments and the publication of results at that level. They do not, therefore, have that much room for manoeuvre, and what they do have is largely negative. If teachers at school level were accountable before the 1970s, they are arguably over-accountable now.

Therefore, for them to exert influence, and to check central government influence, they must act collectively. Unlike parents and governors they are organized collectively already; through their unions. Furthermore, their unions have, as previous chapters have shown, both experience and a variety of means at their disposal for influencing the decision-making process. It is true that during the crisis of the 1980s their power too has been severely curtailed. Nevertheless, the teaching profession remains a highly unionized occupation. If the unions can build on the experience of previous generations, and find effective means of exercising their power in the new context, they will be in a position to provide the necessary check on government's curriculum control. If there is to be across the nation a development of school-level alliances between teachers and the community, then these are only likely to be effective if the teacher organizations provide the leadership, inspiration and organization required. In short, the existence of a healthy, powerful, effective teacher union movement is in the interests not only of teachers and the education service, but also of democracy itself. Ronald Gould argued in 1954:

> I have heard it said that the existence in this country of 146 strong vigorous LEAs safeguards democracy and lessens the risk of dictatorship. No doubt this is true, but an even greater safeguard is the existence of a quarter of a million teachers who are free to decide what should be taught and how it should be taught. (Tropp, 1957, p. 270)

While no one now is demanding such freedom, in terms of responsibility for the future of democracy, Gould's point finds a clear echo almost 40 years later.

Conclusion

In the last section an attempt has been made to sketch, in outline, a possible model of a strategic teacher union. Prior to that, the debate about 'new', 'professional' or 'third generation' unionism was examined in some depth. The times are uncertain, particularly in the education service, and the debate about the future of teacher organizations is in the early stages of a new phase. The preceding sketch is provided against this background and is therefore itself uncertain. Its aim is to contribute to and provide further debate, rather than to bring it to an end.

Two more points may be worth making in conclusion; uncertainty should not be seen as a pretext for doing nothing. On the contrary, the uncertainty and fluidity of the moment provides an opportunity for bold and imaginative action. Finally, I believe the study of the history of the NUT and the analysis of the present state of the education service, if nothing else, makes a powerful case for the existence of effective teachers' organizations prepared to promote the interests of teachers and the education service regardless of the prevailing climate of opinion. A union that began by defeating payment by results and is currently proposing a coherent alternative to the government's crumbling National Curriculum needs no further justification. If teaching has ever been or ever becomes a role of which it is right to have, 'an exalted notion' – as it should be – it will be as a result of the efforts of teacher organizations such as the NUT.

Bibliography

Bachrach, P. and Baratz, M.S. (1962), 'The two faces of power', *American Political Science Review*, 56, pp. 947–85 and 57, pp. 641–51.

Barber, M. (1992), 'An entitlement curriculum', *Journal of Curriculum Studies*, in press.

Batho, G. (1989), *Political Issues in Education*, London, Cassell.

Board of Education (1926), *Report of the Consultative Committee on the Education of the Adolescent* (Hadow Report), London, HMSO.

Board of Education (1931), *Report of the Consultative Committee on the Primary School* (Hadow Report), London, HMSO.

Board of Education (1938), *Report of the Consultative Committee on Secondary Education with Special Reference to Grammar Schools and Technical High Schools* (Spens Report), London, HMSO.

Brown, H. (1979), *The Rise of British Trade Unions, 1825–1914*, London, Longman.

Coates, R. (1972), *Teachers' Unions and Interest Group Politics*, Cambridge, Cambridge University Press.

Cox, C.B. and Dyson, A.E. (eds) (1971), *The Black Papers on Education: A Revised Edition*, London, Davis-Poynter.

Dahl, R.A. (1961), *Who Governs?*, New Haven, CT, Yale University Press.

DES (1972), *Education: A Framework for Expansion*, London, HMSO.

DES (1977), *Education in Schools: A Consultative Document*, London, HMSO.

DES (1981), *Review of the Schools Council* (Trenaman Report), London, DES.

DES (1983), *Teaching Quality*, London, HMSO.

DES (1986), *Report by Her Majesty's Inspectors on the Effects of Local Authority Expenditure Policies on Education in England – 1985*, London, DES.

DES (1989), *National Curriculum: From Policy to Practice*, London, DES.

DES (1990a), *Hackney Free and Parochial Church of England Secondary School, ILEA, 13–15 Dec. 1989*, London, DES.

DES (1990b), *3rd Report of the Interim Advisory Committee on Schoolteachers' Pay and Conditions*, London, HMSO.

DES (1991), *4th Report of the Interim Advisory Committee on School-teachers' Pay and Conditions*, London, HMSO.

DES and Welsh Office (1980), *A Framework for the School Curriculum by the Secretaries of State for Education and Science and for Wales*, London, DES; Cardiff, Welsh Office.

DES and Welsh Office (1985), *Better Schools*, London, HMSO.

DES and Welsh Office (1989), *Discipline in Schools: Report of the Committee of Enquiry Chaired by Lord Elton* (Elton Report), London, DES.

Edwards, B. (1974), *The Burston Strike*, London, Lawrence and Wishart.

Gosden, P.H.J.H. (1972), *The Evolution of a Profession: A Study of the Contribution of Teachers' Associations to the Development of School Teaching as a Professional Occupation*, Oxford, Blackwell.

Ham, C. and Hill, M. (1989), *The Policy Process in the Modern Capitalist State*, Brighton, Wheatsheaf.

Hampshire LEA (1990), *Manual of Personnel Policy and Practice*, Winchester, Hampshire LEA.

Handy, C. (1989), *The Age of Unreason*, London, Hutchinson.

Hewton, E. (1986), *Education in Recession*, London, Allen and Unwin.

ILEA (1976), *William Tyndale Junior and Infant Schools* (Auld Report), London, ILEA.

Jones, K. (1989), Right Turn, London, Hutchinson Radius.

Kerchner, C.E. and Mitchell, D. (1988), *The Changing Idea of a Teachers' Union*, Lewes, Falmer.

Kogan, M. (1975), *Educational Policy-Making*, London, Allen and Unwin.

Kogan, M. (1986a), *Education Accountability: An Analytic Overview*, London, Hutchinson.

Kogan, M. (1986b), *The Politics of Educational Change*, Manchester and London, Manchester University Press.

Lawn, M. (ed.) (1985), *The Politics of Teacher Unionism*, Beckenham, Croom Helm.

Lawn, M. (1987), *Servants of the State*, Lewes, Falmer.

Lawn, M. (1990), *Re-inventing the Polite Trade Union? A New Teacher Unionism for the Nineties in England and Wales*, unpublished paper, Birmingham.

Lawn, M. and Ozga, J. (1981), *Teachers, Professionalism and Class*, Lewes, Falmer.

Lukes, S. (1974), *Power: A Radical View*, London, Macmillan.

Maclure, S. (1989), *Education Reformed: A Guide to the Education Reform Act*, (2nd edn), London, Hodder and Stoughton.

Manzer, R.A. (1970), *Teachers and Politics*, Manchester, Manchester University Press.

Matthews, P. (1989), *Procedures of Consultation and Negotiation in Local*

Education Authorities in England and Wales, unpublished dissertation, University of Manchester.

Morgan, G. (1986), *Images of Organisation*, London, Sage.

Morris, M. and Griggs, G. (eds) (1988), *Education: The Wasted Years? 1973–86*, Brighton, Falmer.

Moser, Sir Claus (1990), *Our Need for an Informed Society*, Presidential Address to the British Association.

NUT (1928), *The Hadow Report and After*, London, NUT.

NUT (1971), *The Teaching Council*, London, NUT.

NUT (1988), *Towards Equality for Girls and Boys*, London, NUT.

NUT (1989a), *Meeting Special Needs in Ordinary Schools*, London, NUT.

NUT (1989b), *Opening Doors*, London, NUT.

NUT (1989c), *Begin at the Beginning*, London, NUT.

NUT (1990a), *A Strategy for the Curriculum*, London, NUT.

NUT (1990b), *NUT/MTA Report*, London, NUT.

NUT (1990c), *Education Review: Managing Education*, 4, No.2, London, NUT.

Pelling, H. (1963), *A History of British Trade Unionism*, Harmondsworth, Penguin.

Plaskow, M. (ed.) (1985), *The Life and Death of the Schools' Council*, Lewes, Falmer.

Roy, W. (1968), *The Teachers' Union*, London, Schoolmaster Publishing Company.

Saran, R. (1985), *The Politics Behind Burnham: A Study of Teachers' Salary Negotiations*, Sheffield, Sheffield City Polytechnic.

School Management Task Force (1989), *Management Development: The Way Forward*, London, DES.

Seifert, R. (1987), *Teacher Militancy*, Lewes, Falmer.

Spaull, A. (1990), *Is There a New Teacher Unionism?*, unpublished AERA paper, Monash University, Australia.

Tropp, A. (1957), *The School Teachers*, London, Heinemann.

Name Index

Subject Index